DICTATOR STYLE

DICTATOR STYLE

LIFESTYLES OF THE WORLD'S MOST COLORFUL DESPOTS

PETER YORK

FOREWORD BY DOUGLAS COUPLAND

CHRONICLE BOOKS

SAN FRANCISCO

First published in the United States in 2006 by Chronicle Books LLC.
First published in Great Britain in 2005 by Atlantic Books, an imprint of
Grove Atlantic Ltd.

Library of Congress Cataloging-in-Publication Data available.
ISBN-10: 0-8118-5314-4
ISBN-13: 978-0-8118-5314-9

Manufactured in China

Book design by Andrew Barker
Jacket design by Tim Belonax

Distributed in Canada by Raincoast Books
9050 Shaughnessy Street
Vancouver, British Columbia V6P 6E5

10 9 8 7 6 5 4 3 2 1

Chronicle Books LLC
85 Second Street
San Francisco, California 94105
www.chroniclebooks.com

CONTENTS

FOREWORD:
TREE FORTS AND LOVE SHACKS

By Douglas Coupland

I remember once seeing a photo of Muammar Gaddafi's master bedroom. It was in *Time* or *Newsweek* and it showed a circular bed with black silk sheets, black headboard – black everything really, including, above the bed, a set of black panther figures of the sort won at a transient funfair arcade. Even to early teenaged eyes, I looked at the photo and thought, 'Hmmmm. Didn't they hire a stylist for this shoot?' The sheets were wrinkled as if the photographer had said, 'Kiki, can you give the sheets a shake out the window? The odor of man musk is a bit overpowering, and for God's sake, don't accidentally inhale a pube.'

What the photo had was *authenticity*. Its rumpled sheets and haphazardly arranged ornaments remind me of a *Hello!* photo shoot I saw a few years later in the 1980s: 'Britt Ekland at Home with Slim Jim Phantom of the Stray Cats'. I remember the photo shoot because you could see the defects and wear patterns in their carpeting and nobody had removed the mundane clutter from a DIY bookcase. Britt and Slim Jim were real, dammit! It was gripping imagery – truly the sort of celebrity-at-home photo that delivers on many levels. Was this even the same photographer who had shot Gaddafi's bedroom? Perhaps. But in Gaddafi's case, what I wanted to see next were the contents of his bedside drawers: Kleenex, Astrolube, a half-eaten kebab and bootleg photos of Henry Kissinger, Jill St. John and Agent X having a three-way in a Davos hotel suite.

Another thing Gaddafi's bedroom reminded me of was the bedrooms of my two older teenaged brothers. If Gaddafi had placed a pyramid of Corona beer bottles on a side table or on the window ledge, my brothers would have fully agreed, and the bottles would have looked in tune with the rest of Gaddafi's love shack. But the thing about bedrooms of adolescent boys and bedrooms of dictators is that (Mussolini aside) there is almost no possibility of their owners ever actually *scoring* in these spaces. Democratically elected politicians prefer to have their sex in swimming-pool cabanas, pantries and limousines paid for by tax-paying citizens of the free world. Sex in the official bedroom? I think not. Imagine Pat Nixon walking in on Richard and Candy, the teenager who got separated from her high school's tour of the White House. It's not going to happen. I suspect the secret language of such dictatorial interiors is almost entirely directed to impress visiting pals rather than, say, young Stacey from the Tripoli Hard Rock Café. *Muammar, don't get your hopes up too high. Yes, she's way out of your league, but what with the silk sheets and the onyx popper dispenser, you might just complete the deal. Wait – did you remember the Frisk mints?*

In this same vein of thought, I remember that my brothers also had a tree fort. There they kept porn, cigarettes and beer in abundance. Girls weren't allowed, but then it's hard to imagine a girl ever wanting in.

My point in all of this is that the psychic dynamics of generic teenage boys in their own spaces and those of dictators at home aren't all that different. Both are dense with assertions of potency and risk-taking: animal skins, posters depicting sci-fi warriors rescuing cheesy sluts from mythical dangerous creatures, the 1978 Farrah Fawcett poster that conquered the planet and . . .

. . . And yet there's a problem here. A dictator's house has to impress the buddies, but it also has to be photographed and shown to the serfs. This results in an interesting clash of needs. *Yes, I'm your dictator who loves and cares for you, the people, but I am also studmaster of the galaxy, a man of taste and education – not a spendthrift* but, rather, a clever and tasteful manipulator of symbolic imagery in a way that befits someone of my massiveness. And for what it's worth, just ignore that Kim Jong-il guy in North Korea – he gives dictators a bad name. What's with those dove-grey pantsuits and those glasses? They make him look like a repeat sex offender.

Pity the poor photographers and stylists who had to take the photographs shown in this book. The year is 1938 and you're working for *Elle Décor's* Berlin edition and suddenly you get summoned to Berchtesgaden. Your instructions? 'We want you to bring out Adolf's playful side. You know – find his joy.' The catch is that you not only have to find Hitler's playful flirty side, but also take photos that show all the folks Hitler grew up with that he's not only powerful but, dammit, he has taste too. But not overly expensive taste – well, okay, maybe it is expensive. That just makes it all the more ghastly and car-crash like. *You see, the thing is, I control the universe and you don't. You can see how I might need – not just want but need – stuffed endangered species surrounding me. They didn't even mind being killed, and I did it ever so gently at that. I broke their necks with my own hands. Okay, Eva broke their necks.*

Unintelligent question from a photographer's assistant: 'Mr. Hitler, would you ever consider stuffing one of your dogs and putting it on display?'

Treblinka, line three.

Here's a scenario: you're on a plane bound for a Romanian getaway. During the flight you buy a *Hello!* magazine with the cover story 'Nicolae Ceausescu: "Welcome to My Charming Gracious Home".' Once on the ground you rent a VW Golf and are on your merry way when, suddenly, a dwarf wino steps in front of the car and is crushed instantly. You're horrified, but nobody seems too concerned and when you leave the police station a long black car awaits you. You hop in and are driven to the Palace. You're to dine with the Ceausescus! Nicolae's first words? 'Thank you for getting rid of that miserable little gymnast. I'd have done it myself except Amnesty International was scrutinizing his movements too closely.'

'Gymnast?'

'Could have made the Olympics but we inspected his dorm room and his radio was set to Radio Free Europe. Hungry?'

You sit down at a dinner table made of gilded Bakelite swans inlaid with medals from what seems to have been one of Michael Jackson's suit jackets. The table seats 36. Nicolae's at one end and you're at the other.

'Madame is in the orphanages tonight dispensing justice to those who require it. Kiki! Bring us our soup right now!'

The soup arrives. It's good. You ask Mr. Ceausescu what it is.

'Cream of protester.'

You run to the main guest bathroom. As it's Eastern Europe, it's difficult to tell which item does what, so, unfortunately, you chunder into Nicolae's personal thermal spa. Your last image before blacking out is the room's wide range of creamy pastel objects. You will never wake up. You will be made into soup.

There is a consistent lesson in all of this. When someone you love gets a bad haircut, no matter how awful it is, you must compliment it. When visiting the homes of dictators, flattery will not only get you anywhere, it will probably save your life. It worked for Kiki.

INTRODUCTION

'In every dream home, a heartache,' goes one of my favorite seventies songs. However rich you are, if you live in a well-governed democracy, planning regulations define what you can build and you need listed-building consent to change old places. The plebs even have the right to roam on your land, as Madonna discovered in Dorset. Sometimes you can't get the architects, the artists, the craftsmen you want for love nor money. The torments of the rich are very real to them; these are things they all moan about. But consider this: *as a full-on dictator, it's all there for you* – the entire resources of your country, the money, the manpower, the artists and craftsmen. No twentieth-century dictator from even the meanest subsistence economy ever had less than a billion dollars at his command. And no dictator has ever had to suffer the building and decoration constraints of the average twenty-first-century Western billionaire. Right to roam? What are Kalashnikovs for? State intervention? *Come on, l'État c'est moi.* Hate that hill, those shacks, that river? That's why they invented dynamite.

As for the subtler constraints of taste, like John Fowler's 'pleasing decay', that have inhibited the traditional upper-classes of England and America for decades, or the dressed-down wooden beams of new Silicon Valley money – the aesthetic of, say, Steven Spielberg or Bill Gates – *all that's for the birds*. The whole point about being a dictator is that you're in a class of one. Like Osbert Lancaster's Lady Littlehampton: 'if it's me it's U'. You're saying it loud for the state, which is you; you're embodying the ancient values of your people (revised in 1930 or 1976 or 1990). It's your taste that counts and, frankly, you're infallible.

You can have houses (or rather palaces) wherever you want. Pick a spot – any spot – and just get building. *You own all spots.* If the spot's peasants object, then your people know what to do. Modern dictators have got the lot: all the powers of the Pharaohs with access to the new technologies of steel framing and glass walls, intelligent lighting, ultra security, sound systems and exotic plumbing.

After a century of totalitarian-model dictators building monuments to the terrifying power of personality, there are now some astonishing exteriors and interiors out there – and a lot of what estate agents call the Wow Factor. I've always been fascinated by the houses of the seriously rich and the deeply important. Forget taste. As the Queen once said, 'It doesn't really help'. What matters is the heady feeling that anything can be done, anything can happen, that all the normal constraints are suspended.

But the *seriously* rich and deeply important have never been anything like as keen to show us their houses as the moderately rich and their siblings in the design classes. The homes of the Great Dictators have always followed the official story (Comrade Stalin posing at home with Soviet children, released by Tass in the 1930s). But we couldn't see Our Beloved Leader's den or his bedrooms and bathrooms. For that – the stuff of the great new international trade in interior photo shoots – we had to wait for him to be deposed or die.

Take Saddam Hussein, a man with roughly 65 palaces by 2003. How did he and his terrifying sons live while the Iraqi economy fell apart under sanctions? What can you learn about his personality and his regime from those places? Masses, it turns out. The pictures alone are extraordinary; quite enough to justify the invasion. As P. J. O'Rourke wrote: 'Saddam's chandelier was the size of a two-car garage. If a reason to invade Iraq was wanted, felony interior decorating would have done.'

Dictators' houses show you what happens when people are left to exercise their fantasies, unrestrained by scale. People with (usually) no training in such things. (Hitler, of course, was a fourth-rate artist and saw himself as a man of taste.) People from overwhelmingly modest backgrounds. People as different as one could imagine from, say, the late John Fowler or Sir Terence Conran or any of the many nice latter-day designers who invite us into their tasteful, quirky, amusing, dressed-down,

GET THE LOOK

These days, every housey-housey magazine and 'shelter publication' on the stands has a 'Get the Look' section. After spreads on the delicious houses of actors, designers and haberdashers there are follow-up strips that tell you 'How-To'. Here are the ten key points of the Dictator Look:

1. BIG IT UP

Make sure that everything is seriously over-scale. If you copy a French chateau, double the size of the rooms.

2. GO REPRO

Dictators like the old style because it looks serious and involves a lot of gold and fancy work. Most of them, however, don't like the real thing — it's too shabby and uncomfortable. Dictators like repro houses and repro furniture in what the eminent English decorator and party inspector Nicky Haslam calls the 'Louis-the-Hotel' style: everything's shiny. (But have you ever seen a piece of top-end eighteenth-century furniture before the sun got to it? It looks utterly gaudy with its bright colored inlays and golden mounts, so who's to say they're wrong?)

3. THINK FRENCH

And while you're in repro mode, *think French*. Repro French decoration and furniture has been the taste of thrusting New Money for 150 years. Cast your mind back to curvy marble chimney pieces, oval-backed gilt chairs and massive commodes covered in golden ormolu. Think of all those *After Boucher* naked-lady paintings in pinky-green oils.

4. THINK HOTEL

Hotels — as shiny as possible — should be your inspiration. Modern dictators have spent a lot of time in hotels — plotting coups there when young and hanging around in them when deposed. For ambitious lads from modest backgrounds, the local grand hotel was always the good-life template. Try to incorporate that Hilton atrium look.

atmospheric houses on a constant basis. Dictators are frankly just like the rest of us. Only more so.

Despite their near infinite resources, most of these dictators haven't exactly produced prize-winning buildings and interiors. They don't go for the liberal Establishment look. Even at their most lurid, they've usually aimed at something pretty conservative and cod-classical. They haven't used the latest construction techniques or employed cutting-edge artists and decorators.

If you want to see the nearest thing to dictator-taste in England, go to Essex and porn-king David Sullivan's huge Lego neo-classical house in Theydon Bois. Or to Bishop's Avenue, the extraordinary Millionaire's Row just beyond Hampstead in north London. The houses there, with their massive 'Tara' porches, are based on multi-ethnic, multi-millionaires' display fantasies. In Los Angeles, just look at TV tycoon Aaron Spelling's huge brand new French chateau in Beverly Hills. Going back a bit, Randolph Hearst's San Simeon, on the Pacific coast halfway between L.A. and San Francisco, is another prime example of Dictator-chic. They're all Outsider entrepreneurs, never part of the Establishment of taste and behavior. The dictators' houses in this book are a bit like theirs — only larger, louder, madder, attesting to the lives lived large inside.

Most of them are completely ghastly to the evolved snobbish eye. So if you like aesthetic *Schadenfreude*, then this book will be a treat. But at the same time the homes in this book are *utterly* compelling. You can't look away. And if you want to contemplate the banality of evil, then here it is, on parade — the homes in this book are failures of imagination: shiny surfaces and effects remembered from bad films and even worse hotels. Plus occasional concessions to *gemütlich* and other man-of-the-people poses. Whether you think these interiors are terrible or,

5. GO FOR GOLD (STARTING WITH TAPS)

Gold is good and gold taps are everywhere. From Ceausescu to Saddam Hussein it's a staple of the style. Gold taps say *I've got money and I don't care what people think*. Gold taps – not usually 'real' gold but a special variant of lacquered alloy – come from bathroom shops in Mayfair, London who specialize in the style. Try South Audley Street.

6. GET MORE GLASS

Chandeliers are the diamonds of interior decoration. Glittering away against massive mirrors, they give the Ferrero Rocher look instantly.

7. HAVE IMPORTANT NINETEENTH-CENTURY OILS

Immaculately finished pot-boilers turned out by nineteenth-century salon painters have found a second home in dictator-land. The 'Art Pompier' painted for the made-its of 1850s Leeds or Lyons really looks the business; much better than some of those grim Old Masters.

8. INVOLVE BRANDS

Known Value Items. You've got the Mercedes out front (at least ten of them), so do the same indoors. Go Ming. Go Aubusson. Choose names people know, objects you can talk about, pieces with a price (since the early 1990s that's meant Go Versace too).

9. MAKE IT MARBLE

Involve as much marble as possible. New marble, obviously, as the old stuff can be distinctly manky. It has to be tremendously figured, not the plain kind architects favor, and it has to be high-gloss, not 'honed' or 'distressed' or any of those pointless stealth-wealth things.

10. HAVE YOURSELF EVERYWHERE

Whether it's Hitler's pallid face emerging from the dark in the portrait in his Berlin apartment, a similar portrait of Mussolini in his study to put you off your supper, Mrs. Marcos rising from the waves or Mrs. Ceausescu graduating from university, celebrate your achievements. You're doing it for the people (but make sure it's *on-myth*).

---

secretly, rather inspirational, one thing is certain: none of them is beige. Somewhere in there is a lesson for us all.

Halfway through this book my editor asked me to cut down on 'hideous' and 'ugly'. I'd over-used them, he said. Wasn't that just lazy writing? (And couldn't my reaction be read as rather Western middle-class and unimaginative?) He's right, of course, but there's a lot here that is hideous and ugly. If you try to think yourself into these houses – and it's hard – the key word is *wretched*. Forget taste entirely; many of these houses feel miserable. They are bent out of shape by driven, distorted people. The display principle is absolutely central – not just Wotalotigot, but power and intimidation too. Nothing looks remotely comfortable. With Saddam's 'palaces' you get the feeling that nothing really works properly. Mrs. Marcos's bedroom is the epitome of 1940s glamor from a film set, an incomplete show-house with no ergonomics at all.

It's no coincidence the 'Hotel Look' is so popular with dictators. The boundaries between public and private aren't clear for them. Many of the rooms you're about to see are public, for meetings as much as families and the look is as much about manipulation as aspiration, and the paranoia is dripping from the walls. Dictators all seem to have especially paranoid personalities (though that doesn't mean people aren't trying to get them). Paranoia was Stalin's organizing principle, translated into get-them-before-they-get-you and 'death solves all problems'. So you have guards inside and out, a barracks behind the house and every bit of new security technology you can find. And still you're jumpy.

At its most extreme – in Saddam Hussein's case, for example – you don't actually sleep in the palace you've used for that day's meetings; you move to a much more modest safe house. Meanwhile, dinner is cooked and served to lookalikes in palaces all over the country. Let them get shot instead.

Very few of these men inherited more than a row of beans. They'd had no training in the Duke of Devonshire side of things. And no time either. No dictator in his prime gave a moment's thought to *work–life balance*. These were men who'd been on the run, lived rough and served prison sentences before they made it; and they often had to do it all again after they were deposed. Who will forget Saddam Hussein crawling out of a filthy hole in the ground in 2003?

A dictator's chances of dying comfortably in bed are also considerably lower than average. It's a very tough game, so the other obvious comparison is with major career criminals. You don't feel safe unless you've got your tribe or your gang around you. Government by cronies – actually the heavy mob from your village – is central to the dictatorial lifestyle. So dictators don't grow up into classic, companionate marriages, they never get private lives; they're always hanging out with the boys. Unless, of course, they've got the Lady Macbeth She-Devil to work with, like Ceausescu or Milosevic (Imelda Marcos was something else again, but certainly a big part of that political operation).

DICTATOR STYLE

PORFIRIO DÍAZ

This rather narrow boudoir is actually the presidential train of Porfirio Díaz, President of Mexico from 1877 to 1911 and the first leader to be widely termed 'Dictator'. As a convinced modernizer, like England's Prince Albert, railways were hugely important to Díaz. During his time in power he increased the railway network in Mexico tenfold, encouraged foreign investment and successfully created an industrial base in a peasant economy. Queen Victoria also had her own train. It carried her corpse (and all the grieving crowned heads of Europe) on her final journey from London to Windsor in 1901.

An enthusiasm for railway travel may be Victorian, but Díaz's carriage is more suggestive of the kind of Texan whorehouse we see in Westerns. It is smothered in textiles: silk damask upholstery, squishy cushions, elaborate fringing, and there's a raised ceiling with fanciful stencilling and small arched windows inset in the roof – the sort of thing you might find in a traditional nineteenth-century sunroom. There's a large oval mirror in the panelling, a lot of shiny wood and a hanging brass lamp. It's ideal for the secret assignations of an elderly Latin American soldier who liked to play away from home.

Díaz sold off great chunks of Mexico to foreign investors at the expense of health, longevity and social justice – not unlike England circa 1850. There was never any redistribution of wealth – quite the opposite. Díaz's pact with the land-owners enabled them to take over common land in the knowledge that Díaz's crack squads of former bandits would soon put down any peasant protests.

Díaz's opponents said that he tried to develop Mexico too fast and sold out to foreign investors. As he got older (he was 80 when he was deposed), he became too obviously partisan towards the modernizers, which alienated Mexico's provincial elite. Díaz died in exile in Paris. It was a humiliating end for a perpetual president who managed to move Mexico so far onto the agenda of the early twentieth-century world that Victoria's son Edward VII made him an honorary Grand Commander of the Bath in 1906.

FULL NAME
José de la Cruz Porfirio Díaz Mori

TITLE
President of Mexico

YEARS IN POWER
1877–80, 1884–1911 (left office 1880–4 due to term limit)

VLADIMIR LENIN

Everything about Lenin was re-worked after he died. Most famously, his body was preserved – and some said re-made in wax – by the Soviet authorities. Dictators and their families, from Peron to Mrs. Marcos, have always appreciated the value of an embalmed holy relic.

The Soviet history books were re-written on Stalin's orders to show him and Lenin as life-long friends – and to portray Stalin as Lenin's natural successor. Lenin's long death-bed Testament (in which he criticized Stalin) was suppressed and early photographs of the leaders of the Revolution were airbrushed to eliminate rivals like Leon Trotsky. So it's only natural to be suspicious about these interior shots of Lenin's home. Aren't his Moscow quarters just a little bit too sparse and ascetic? Perhaps he was really living in luxury elsewhere and this was all reconstructed by the Soviet equivalent of Ralph Lauren's set dressers.

The rest home that Lenin used at Gorky – known as the Big House – was a very different affair. These photographs show a late eighteenth-century, upper-class, classical house with beautiful views – the kind of place you could see Tolstoy living in, rather than the father of Marxism-Leninism, the leader of the Bolshevik Revolution, the creator of the world's first socialist state and the godfather of every communist revolutionary that followed him in Europe, Asia and Africa.

In fact, both of Lenin's houses and styles make perfect sense. First we have the Kremlin quarters of a childless, left-wing intellectual after the Revolution. The plain parquet floor, the high ceilings and the grand piano in the drawing room are typical late nineteenth-century. Converted from part of the Kremlin, the flat is a fragment of the *ancien régime*, stripped down for a cultivated intellectual who was too busy for home comforts. His wife and fellow Marxist, Nadezhda Krupskaya, and his sister, Maria, also lived here.

The dining room (*opposite*) is sparse but almost elegant – not unlike the homes of Lenin's Western contemporaries.

FULL NAME
Vladimir Ilich Ulyanov

TITLES
Chairman of the Soviet of People's Commissars; Premier of the Soviet Union

INFAMOUS MONIKER
Lenin (possibly named after the Lena River)

YEARS IN POWER
1917–24

FAMILY

wife: **Nadezhda Konstantinovna Krupskaya**

The table is bare; the furniture is anonymous. But the ceiling height, the quality of the joinery on the white partition and the rather Arts-and-Crafts-looking border below the cornice all have an undeniable flair. In Lenin's bedroom (*page 6*), there's a plain brass single bed – almost child size – a side table and a lamp. The pedestal desk has a pre-Revolutionary Edwardian look, while the desk chair seems like something from Thonet's bent-wood factory – a cult with early twentieth-century intellectuals before Modernism. The two other plain chairs have seats and backs in leather, embossed as the fashionable crocodile. Hung pointedly above the bed is a photograph of Lenin and his wife looking comradely in their hats.

In contrast, the Big House at Gorky (*opposite*) comes straight out of a *World of Interiors* spread on, say, a Russian writer's house or even a Swedish toff's house circa 1800 – there's a touch of the fashionable Gustavians in the elegant white and gold furniture, and the striped, loose-covered chairs make it look like the set of a Chekhov play. It's recognizably aspirational: the big old country house bathed in perpetual sunlight. There's more old parquet floor here and a Frenchified Napoleonic strip of carpet in the foreground (pre-Revolutionary upper-class Russians spoke French). The corner window in this drawing room looks out onto a stone balustrade with trees beyond. This room is clearly grand, but it's not royal. Once a typical gentry pad, the Big House was nationalized in 1918 and was available for Lenin's convalescence after an assassination attempt left two bullets lodged inside him. It remained his country retreat until his death in 1924.

Lenin's Big House is much more in keeping with his real origins than the Soviet airbrushers wanted to admit. He was deeply bourgeois – certainly not a sturdy peasant like Stalin. Lenin was from that slice of the senior bureaucratic middle class that bordered on the gentry in late nineteenth-century Russia. His mother inherited a share in his grandfather's small country estate, where Lenin stayed as a boy (and where the estate manager drove hard bargains with the peasantry). A straight-A student at school and a law graduate from St. Petersburg University, he spoke several languages, read widely and travelled extensively. He was perfectly equipped to move up into the Big House, thereby fulfilling his well-connected mother's aspirations.

The Big House became Lenin's HQ as his health deteriorated from 1922 onwards. He had inherited a tendency to strokes and was possibly suffering from the final stages of syphilis (though this was suppressed at the time). Whatever the diagnosis, this became the home of an invalid. Lenin wrote his political Testament when he could, but much of the time he was bedridden.

Lenin's final home was the Mausoleum in Moscow's Red Square. For the next sixty-five years, he received the faithful in their millions. They say it's rather quieter there now.

JOSEPH STALIN

FULL NAME
Joseph Vissarionovich Dzhughashvili

TITLES
People's Commissar for Nationalities; People's Commissar for Workers' and Peasants' Inspection; General Secretary of the Soviet Communist Party

INFAMOUS MONIKER
Stalin, 'Man of Steel'

YEARS IN POWER
1922–53

FAMILY
first wife: **Ketevan Svanidze;** son: **Yakov Dzhughashvili;**
second wife: **Nadezhda Allilueva;** son: **Vassili;**
daughter: **Svetlana**

This was once the most famous hovel in the world (*opposite*). It's Stalin's birthplace in Georgia, celebrated in fawning hagiographies of all kinds – books, newspapers, magazines – and in Soviet Realist paintings, mass-produced in their millions from 1933 to 1953.

This wretched place showed beyond doubt Stalin's proletarian credentials. He'd had it tough, and millions of Russians who had it tougher still under Stalin could identify with this background. It differed considerably from those of many of the original bourgeois revolutionaries of the early 1920s, such as Trotsky and even Lenin himself (although as a dying saint of the Revolution, history was re-written to cast Lenin as an honorary prole). This shack, and the heavily doctored family story that went with it, was part of Stalin's claim to Soviet authenticity, which he used successfully to win the leadership struggle.

Stalin's presentation of himself as a 'man of the people' was based on some truth. The 'coarseness' of his behavior used to offend Lenin, while his strong Georgian

accent and the unimpressive style of his speeches led to him being described initially as a 'grey blur'. His short stocky body, thick hair and pock-marked face (always airbrushed in contemporary Soviet photographs) seemed deeply and reassuringly ordinary, like his clothes which, in the early days at least, were consistently worker-revolutionary in style. But that was as far as it went. Education in a seminary, interrupted by a short spell in a shoe factory (which he loathed), voracious reading and, above all, 17 years – much of it on the run – devoted to revolutionary politics made for a very un-ordinary human being.

Stalin was not remotely sentimental about the working classes. After the Revolution he spent as little time as possible visiting factories or coal mines. He could leave that kind of propaganda to the Soviet Realist artists, who often showed Comrade Stalin in humble scenes surrounded by adoring workers.

Stalin wasn't interested in having a show house – unlike Hitler, who was fascinated by the theatricalities of Albert Speer's public architecture and proud of his own rather mimsy home in the Berghof. In contrast, Stalin's houses are practical places with no pretensions to elegance or self-expression. They are private and rather secretive (and in this sense completely 'on message'). He usually slept on plain single divans, either in his office or in sitting rooms – even in his bedroom in his married quarters at the Kremlin, because he and his second wife, Nadezhda Allilueva, kept such different hours. After her suicide in 1934, Stalin lived the life of a political bachelor – gregarious, certainly not celibate, fond of staying up late with old friends and cronies and unhindered by family life. He lived in a climate of intense political paranoia so privacy was essential. Secret debates, negotiations and assassination plots all took place at home.

After Nadezhda's death, Stalin lived predominantly in an apartment in the Yellow Palace, just one floor below his Kremlin office, and in a newly built dacha at Kuntsevo (opposite, top), five miles away and easily reached from central Moscow. There were, of course, a number of other places – holiday homes and former Romanov houses – that Stalin kept staffed and guarded. In fact, during his 20 years as undisputed ruler of the U.S.S.R.,

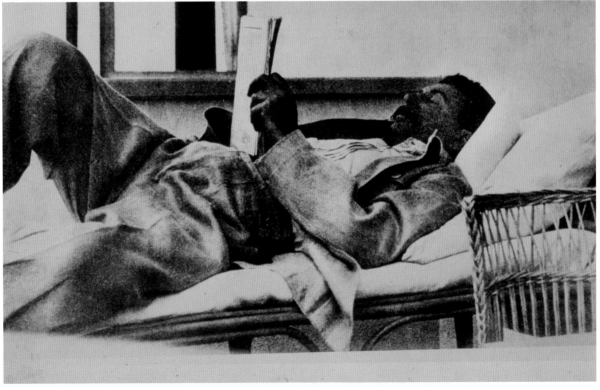

JOSEPH STALIN

the number and scale of his houses grew exponentially. But the style didn't change.

The Kremlin apartment was, apparently, a somber place with high vaulted ceilings. Simon Sebag Montefiore quotes Stalin's daughter, Svetlana, who wrote that 'It was not like a home.' Kuntsevo, on the other hand, was spacious and modern. It was designed (like many of the dachas) by Stalin's court architect, Miron Merzhanov. Like Hitler's small mountain chalet, Stalin's one-story Kuntsevo home soon acquired a second level. And just like Hitler's Berghof, Stalin's country home became a complex with the guest villas, security guardhouses and innumerable checkpoints watched over by at least a hundred guards. This pattern of large and imposing – though unpretentious – camouflage green – painted houses in high-security encampments was repeated elsewhere around Russia, including the Black Sea resort towns of Sochi and Gagra.

Stalin's favorite holiday home, the dacha at Kholodnaya Rechka in the hills near Gagra on the Black Sea, was rebuilt in the 1930s. The garden front (*page 11*) looks curiously old-fashioned; if it were in Western Europe its pediments, pilasters and windows would have been typical of the early 1900s (in England it would be called middle-class Edwardian). The setting is spectacular; the garden is pleasant but barely landscaped. There may not have been impressive facades and smart furnishings in Stalin's houses, but they were built and rebuilt to meet his need for increasingly large dining spaces – for those interminable dinners during which Stalin would cajole, banter with and humiliate his lieutenants – as well as cinemas and billiard rooms.

Stalin liked to work in the gardens of his dachas – planting – and would read and eat outside, seated at wicker tables. He was photographed there by Vasily, his bodyguard. The shot of Stalin (*page 13*) sprawled out on a wicker day-bed, reading his newspaper, one leg bent, is startling in its intimacy. By the 1930s conventions of dictator-photography, this is *lèse-majesté*: rumpled, over-relaxed and not 'properly' composed.

On Stalin's desk in his dacha at Zelyenaya Roshcha (Green Grove), is this curious set (*opposite, top*). It was a gift to Stalin from the Chinese communist leader Mao Tse Tung. But a *desk set* is inherently un-Chinese and, for that matter, deeply bourgeois. It is ideologically and ethnically suspect; it doesn't fit the design vernacular any which way. One can only guess at the functions of these various objects, but somewhere in there is a device big enough to hold the box of matches for lighting Stalin's pipe (shown in the foreground).

This bunker (*opposite, bottom*) is Stalin's emergency cabinet room. At one end is a portrait – perhaps of Lenin? – and to either side are apparently pointless chimney pieces. Nice parquet floor. If all else fails they can have their Final Dinner here.

BENITO MUSSOLINI

Here's Benito Mussolini – a.k.a. Il Duce ('The Leader') – hard at work in his gigantic office in the Palazzo Venezia in Rome. This impressive fifteenth-century palace was once the embassy of the Venetian Republic and is now a national museum. Mussolini is in the Sala de Mappamondo or globe room, which contains a huge wooden globe made by Amanzio Maroncelli in 1722. This room is enormous – 60 feet long, 40 feet wide and 40 feet high. However, all it contained in Mussolini's time was this large table that he used as a desk and a few chairs. Out of sight to the right is a huge chimney piece and above that, set in a curious triangular frame, is an equally huge *fasces* – a bundle of rods with a projecting ax blade, the emblem of Italian Fascism.

Mussolini's office is a gesture of scale, just like Hitler's Chancellery in Berlin. It's a massive empty room. Both looked like 1930s film sets – you could imagine the huge columns were marbled plaster, that the decoration was all *tromped* to the max and that a few feet above the cornice there were those big old blinkered lights on gantries. However, this office is the real deal. It's an old Italian aristocratic bravura thing. There's old marble everywhere: a pictorial floor in colored marbles, marble slabs up the walls. . . . Marble working is a particularly Italian art. It's all real, but it still looks like a scene from *Citizen Kane*.

Mussolini and Hitler had similar delusions of grandeur, but with one crucial difference: the Palazzo Venezia is the lair of a love-god. Quinto Navarra, Il Duce's man-servant, says that Mussolini had sex with a different woman almost every single day from September 1929 until the collapse of the Fascist regime in July 1943. Thousands of loyal signorinas wrote to Mussolini – their short, bald, virile dictator – offering themselves, and his staff sorted out the sweetest. As Sylvia Plath once said, 'Every woman adores a Fascist.' These saucy assignations took place here in the late afternoon, tightly scheduled between Il Duce's official audiences. According to Nicholas Farrell, Mussolini's biographer: 'The love-making took place on a stone window seat, against a wall or on a carpet and was rapid. Once over, Mussolini would dismiss the women immediately without even offering them coffee, liqueur or even a piece of cake.'

This is also the place where Mussolini and Clara Petacci, his mistress, first became lovers in 1936. She was with Mussolini when he was captured by Italian partisans in 1945. Although Clara was offered the chance to escape, she chose to stay. They were shot and their bodies hung upside down at an Esso petrol station, where the crowd beat the corpses.

Mussolini's writing desk was tidy. He used red and blue pencils to mark up the mass of paperwork – newspapers, intelligence reports – that he went through every day. As a successful former journalist he read and filed *everything*. The gilt-brass lamp is spectacularly hefty, with its claw feet. Converted to electricity, with a very 1930s balloon shade and beaded fringe, it looks curiously anachronistic in that grand space. In fact, Mussolini got into the habit of leaving the lights on in his office all night, which earned him the nickname the 'Sleepless One'.

Here's another workspace (*opposite*): Mussolini's home office in the Villa Torlonia. The table and chairs look sixteenth-century and may well be genuine – the fireplace is massive. Like the study in the Palazzo Venezia, this room is big and bare. A portrait of Il Duce glares at us, his huge Roman head looming out of the darkness. This portrait style echoes the portrait of Hitler in his Berlin flat (see *page vi*). This kind of portraiture is a crucial part of the dictator's repertoire. I suspect it'll be read differently by different generations – genuinely scary in the 1930s, it reads as rather *Twilight Zone* now.

The Villa Torlonia was a great folly. It was begun in the sixteenth century, then rebuilt in the early nineteenth century by the Torlonia banking family. Around the central core of a nineteenth-century neo-classical villa are 13 very un-Roman 'constructions', including a Swiss House, a Princes House and a Moresque greenhouse. Outside are Egyptian-style obelisks, statues and columns. The then Prince Torlonia (a committed Mussolini fan who lived in the Owl Palace, another folly on the estate) let Il Duce have the villa from 1929 to 1943 for a rent of one lira a year.

Mussolini's family lived here too: his wife Rachele – the home-town girl whose mother had been Mussolini's father's mistress – and their five children. A woman of simple tastes, Donna Rachele varnished the antique furniture and put up frilly lace curtains. She turned part of the park into a farm with vegetables, livestock, dovecotes and kennels – plus lion cubs, a jaguar, a monkey and other exotic animals and birds given to Il Duce as tributes.

Rachele often shouted at her husband and mocked him in front of the children. In fact, Mussolini's domestic arrangements – a hot-tempered wife, several mistresses, five children and a farm – are so stereotypical they could be taken from an Italian sitcom or a pasta sauce commercial, rather than from the private life of a brutal Fascist dictator.

What could be more natural for Il Duce than Roman kitsch? It was a reassuring resource, readily on hand and favored by Napoleon. Italian Fascists loved kitsch. For instance, Mussolini's outsized head was exploited in Roman portraits and medallions. As part of Mussolini home-dec, this cradle (*right, and detail opposite*) is somewhere between Gianni Versace's home collection (cod classical to the max) and the heft of Bugatti furniture. Made for Il Duce's youngest son, it combines the theatrical gilded eagle prow (a sort of boat on legs) with the solidity of the best nineteenth-century furniture, from a single block of wood. It must weigh a ton. Presumably the metal strut at the back was to stretch white linen over when Mussolini Junior was out in the sun.

Like the Nazis, the Italian Fascists worked hard to achieve a consistent look in their buildings, interiors, uniforms, paintings, sculptures and graphics – a kind of Fascist brand identity. Everything they touched took on a debased operatic quality. The most impressive example – built at a time when Italy was regarded as the world leader in hard masculine Futurist design – is probably Milan Railway Station. The ambitious scale of its great hall and its hideous over-blown symbolism are almost redeemed by its practical and democratic purpose. Say what you like about Mussolini, he made the trains run on time.

ADOLF HITLER

The Berghof, Adolf Hitler's alpine retreat, is 1,200 feet above Berchtesgaden in the Bavarian Alps. It looks like an early Bond film setting. There are postcard views that look kitschy, almost ironic to a twenty-first-century eye. It's a villain's aerie, an eagle's nest.

The Berghof looked out over Austria from three sides: the Führer's homeland as viewed from the Fatherland. These views from the terrace are what you see in all those *Hitler in Colour* documentaries. The British Prime Minister Neville Chamberlain came here for the 'Peace in our Time' meeting in 1938. He probably stood on the terrace thinking 'That Herr Hitler is a bit *intense*.'

The Berghof was originally very *volk*: a three-bedroom mountain lodge called Haus Wachenfeld, which Hitler had first rented in 1927. He then bought it and had it enlarged and remodelled as the center of a massive Nazi complex. The Obersalzburg (literally, Over-Salzburg) hill was alive with the sound of construction in the mid-1930s. Around the Berghof were houses for Hermann Göring (who established the Gestapo and directed the development of the Luftwaffe) and Martin Bormann (Hitler's private secretary), as well as a hotel, an SS barracks and kindergartens for staff children. The area was fenced off – a sort of *gated* compound – and the ordinary *volk* houses cleared away.

It's all gone now, bombed by the RAF in 1945 and the remainder blown up by the Germans in 1952 as a tremendous embarrassment. We're looking at a vanished interior here; one in which the Nazi hierarchy would have discussed the *Anschluss*, the takeover of Austria and the invasion of Poland.

Inside, the décor is anything but Ken Adam – the production designer on several Bond films, whose family left Germany in 1934 to avoid the Nazis. It's actually more like 1920s fumed oak from suburban Surrey; anxiously 'tasteful', but on a large scale, crossed in some places with a kind of invented Bavarian vernacular (the heavily vaulted whitewashed corridors, the arched oak

FULL NAME
Adolf Hitler

TITLES
Führer und Reichkanzler (Leader and Imperial Chancellor); President of the National Socialist German Workers' Party (NSDAP), or Nazi Party

INFAMOUS MONIKER
Der Führer

YEARS IN POWER
1933–45

FAMILY
wife: **Eva Braun**

double doors and the knotty pine panelling). They symbolize Hitler's view of the strong simple yearnings of the South German people.

The location and style are important. The undeniably beautiful setting gives historic and mythological legitimacy to a whole mass of ideas about German destiny. It was as potent an image for the Nazis as, say, a stately home and a Capability Brown landscape would have been for a British audience in the 1930s. This sort of thing evokes every kind of collective unconscious reaction from German Romantic painting (Caspar David Friedrich) to Wagner (is *this* Valhalla?).

The house itself fits a key archetype. By the time these photographs were taken, it was impressively large in terms of the number of rooms (guest annexes of bedrooms) and the scale of some of them. Yet it had an unimpressive facade in a mountainside, and the gardens were naturalistic rather than formal. It remained a fantastically overgrown version of the small mountain lodge it once was. It's strong, almost comically austere and 'manly'; the house of a warrior (which is stretching things a little for an unfit obsessive like Hitler, who we know was hopeless at relating to grown women).

The hall (*page 30*) could easily be in a monastery. This is clearly a bachelor's home, not a family one. It's somewhere great plans are developed. It's somewhere for hunting or skiing or anything done in comparative isolation from the decadence of the city. It's all in line with Hitler's own asceticism and high profile – he didn't drink or smoke and was vegetarian. However, his key lieutenants weren't at all ascetic and there were elaborate dinners, good wine and smoke-filled rooms. You imagine the Führer going to bed early on those nights.

For Hitler himself, the Berghof was an important reward. It was the only house, so he said, that he ever personally owned and it was certainly the only one that expressed his taste. The Berghof was the answer to years of humiliation and rejection in Austria, living in hostels, even sleeping rough – the story he dramatized in *Mein Kampf*, his manifesto-biography of 1925, which had sold over eight million copies by 1945 (the German government alone bought six million copies, and it was their generous gift to all German newlyweds). In the Berghof Hitler

presented himself as he wanted. Here he could entertain on his own terms – flying in artists and musicians who had to acknowledge his power. In the Berghof he could identify his own struggle and achievement with the German nation's historic struggle.

The study (*page 23*) is intended to show Hitler as Man of Destiny as well as Man of Culture (he was a wannabe artist and a wannabe architect, though actually little better than a pavement artist in Vienna). The bookshelves, inset in pitch-pine panelling (out of shot), hold what appear to be new, unread sets of the *Encyclopedia Britannica*. The furniture looks new, too: heavy in a vaguely Black Forest-trad style. The pictures on the walls remind one of nineteenth-century potboilers in machine-gilt composition frames.

The Great Room (*opposite, below*) looks like a hotel. Above the piano is probably the best thing in the house: a real Gobelin tapestry. Was it looted from somewhere – or did the Ministry of Works equivalent in Berlin keep stock for government buildings? Leaning against the wall in the drawing room (*opposite top, and overleaf*) are more unplaceable landscapes. One offers a nasty Symbolist view of the sunlit uplands of the next hill; the other is a nineteenth-century *Rocky Cove with Sailing Boat*, that staple of the secondary salesrooms.

In another corner of the drawing room, looking grouped for the camera, is a Louis-the-hotel table with what appear to be those mimsy nineteenth-century mock-eighteenth-century German porcelain figurines – Dresden, not Meissen – and rather oddly, a silver dressing table set. Very ladylike. Very Hyacinth Bucket.

Did Unity Mitford come here? Did the Windsors? As mad and fascist-loving as so many of Hitler's English society fans were, wouldn't Hitler's house have struck them as more than a bit ridiculous and (in Nancy Mitford's terms) quite Shriekingly Non-U? And where did Hitler get the idea? Is this the sort of thing he saw when he was first 'taken up' by the Munich rich – people like the Bechstein piano family?

Nevertheless, all of the symbolism in the Berghof was completely right for the German public, who saw these images – most of them by Heinrich Hoffmann, Hitler's trusted personal photographer – in newspapers and

magazines throughout the late 1930s. The simple Bavarian resonances, the petit bourgeois detailing – the complete avoidance of any of the demonized 'decadent' styles – will have struck just the right note. There's no *ancien régime* aristocratic elegance, no metropolitan Art Deco chic (the Nazis railed against Hollywood, with its Jews and homosexuals); above all not a trace of Modernism, which was regarded by the Nazis as the style of the communist intelligentsia.

The Berghof does its job, just like Hitler's office, the intimidating Berlin Chancellery. In *The Edifice Complex*, the architectural critic Deyan Sudjic describes it as an over-sized film-set representation of Nazi power, confidence and world domination, which was actually arranged, film style, as an enfilade for the camera, with the whole building just one vast deep room.

This isn't the first time Hitler's Berghof has been written up by an Englishman. As late as November 1938 – less than a year before Britain declared war on Germany – *Homes and Gardens* magazine ran a breathless piece by the oddly named Ignatius Phayre, which treated Hitler like an A-list actor with a heavy schedule. It's a reminder of just how, even then, so many socially smart people in England seemed to think Herr Hitler was a pretty decent guy, if a bit strict and shouty.

'It *had* to be close to the Austrian border,' declares Phayre archly. He was told that the massive sales of Hitler's book *Mein Kampf* paid for the place. And then there's the real kicker: 'In this matter he has throughout been his own architect. . . .' Hitler applied to art and architecture schools in Vienna and was rejected by both. We know from contemporary evidence and from Albert Speer's diaries that Hitler was fascinated by architectural effects. He was obsessed with the stagey and the mytho-logical, with facades and streetscapes, but he lacked the application to design a building or even the ability to draw the detailing. Did he really work out the vaulting in those wide corridors and its relationship to the hefty central column – or did he leave it to Speer or the builders?

Berghof isn't just a statement of traditional Bavarian styles. It's a personal one-in-the-eye for those arty bourgeois Viennese who rejected a socially gauche,

unskilled provincial boy from Linz with a starey expression and an almost epileptic tendency to rant. For Hitler, the design credits for the Berghof were a hugely important vindication.

Phayre goes on to note how Hitler's study was fitted as a modern office with a telephone exchange leading out of it. This initial impression of a Command Center isn't wrong. From that exchange, Hitler could invite his smart Eurotrash friends or ministers to fly over to Berchtesgaden. They landed at Hitler's personal airfield, just below the chalet lawns. In 1930s terms, it was fantastically modern and aircraft were an important part of Hitler's daily life. His own pilot, Hansel Baur, brought him the national and foreign newspapers every day.

The color scheme throughout the Berghof, according to Phayre, was a light jade green. Hitler, he claims, was his own decorator, designer and furnisher as well as architect. He was forever building on new guest-annexes and arranging his favorite antiques. Apparently, Munich antique dealers were briefed to find German eighteenth-century furniture for him. Yet there isn't much to show for it, and what *is* in any recognizable antique style looks fake – what salesrooms call 'of recent manufacture' or the kind of over-decorated stuff ('some parts eighteenth-century') that dealers palmed off on pretentious types in the 1930s.

Those new guest-bedrooms, predictably enough, were decorated in parochial style, hung with old engravings but also *with Hitler's own water-color sketches* (I've never seen one up close, but they look pretty hopeless in reproduction). The late Marquis of Bath – something of a Führer fan by all accounts – was said to have had a fair collection of Hitler's work.

The 'Sun Parlor' (*opposite, bottom*) is definitely suburban Surrey, with its rubber plant, wicker chair, trolley, potted plants and Hartz mountain canary. There's a department-store standard lamp with a segmental 'parchment' shade and a mock-1820s central light fitting. Unlike the other rooms it looks terribly unplanned. This could be an Enid Blyton setting, a *Daily Express* Rupert Bear bolt-hole, or somewhere for Richmal Crompton's Just William to apologize. The other parlor (*opposite, top*) is hideous. Net curtains, potted plants, a particularly nasty

long case clock, a frilly lamp shade and the worst kind of 'traditional' parlor chairs (if they were antique in 1935, I'm a banana) with rounded backs, splayed 'bobbin' legs and sticky brown-Windsor varnish you can see across 70 years. There also seems to be a swastika cushion in the windowseat. I don't believe anyone in Hitler's ménage did Fake London-type irony for a moment. I think it's a folded banner or poster, but in this setting it looks decidedly creepy.

JOSIP BROZ TITO

Tito's achievement was amazing. He pulled together a range of Balkan blood feuds – Serbs, Croats and Muslims – into a modern nation. He ran a 'third way' communist country successfully from the end of the Second World War until 1980, playing East and West against each other and creating relative prosperity (by Eastern European standards) along the way. But if Yugoslavia was born out of idealism – and Tito's ruthless pragmatism – it was also the home of the New Class: communists who ate Godiva chocolates.

Tito's wartime collaborator and former vice-president Milovan Djilas, a long-term idealist, intellectual and writer, described this communist 'New Class' in his 1957 book. His argument applied to the entire Eastern Bloc, though his description of a new aristocracy in communist countries sounded a lot like home. He talked about people with big flats and houses, expensive cars and chauffeurs, people who had a shoo-in to the best education for their children and were guaranteed access to otherwise unobtainable Western luxuries – imported food and wine, clothes and cosmetics. Nothing was too good for Yugoslav communism's top people, the *nomenklatura*, the office holders. The pigs had taken over the farm and were walking on their hind legs.

This picture (*opposite*) shows the power of office: the huge nineteenth-century desk of state hideously over-carved from sticky, dark brown-Windsor stained wood – possibly the Balkan equivalent of bog oak – with the books and the sort of desk furniture that captains of industry from another age were always being given: marble and onyx desk-sets, pens in precious metals (see Stalin). Behind Tito, festering away, there's an 'important' picture with a dark opera-chorus of characters. There's a round rug and some serious-looking wallpaper to set it off. Tito is dressed in full uniform, but he seems, as in all of these pictures, more than a little out of it.

As Djilas showed, the state didn't wither away, leaving the working class to run the show. The New Class had the

FULL NAME
Josip Broz

TITLE
President of Yugoslavia

INFAMOUS MONIKER
Tito

YEARS IN POWER
1945–80

FAMILY
first wife: **Marusa Novakova;** son: **Leopard Novakov**
second wife: **Pelagija Belousova;** son: **Zarko Broz**
third wife: **Elza Gerlach;** son: **Viktor Gerlach**
fourth wife: **Zuhra Reuf-Anadolka;** son: **Izet Reuf**
fifth wife: **Davorjanka Paunovic-Zdenka;** son: **Slavisa Paunovic**
sixth wife: **Jovanka Broz**

opposite effect. The state grew bigger because it had to control absolutely everything and everybody – and the people at the top had to bring in all those Great Leaps Forward, Five-Year Plans and revolutions within the Revolution. A host of bureaucratic chores would keep them occupied for decades. They established themselves as a kind of unofficial new aristocracy – with a set of privileges that extended to their children, and sometimes grandchildren, and which were put on display in their eminently comfortable homes.

Djilas's New Class was made up of 'those who have special privileges and economic preference because of the administrative monopoly they hold'. In the 1930s, he tells us, the wages of the average Soviet industrial worker and those of a very junior provincial member of the New Class differed by a multiple of 25. So how much more did the top bosses cream off in the 1950s, when any rewards or perks would be kept secret for decades? Salary was the least of it. Houses were commandeered all over the place from naughty aristos and old-order plutocrats; cars and drivers were charged to the state and household staff were

written off as factory workers. Communism created an entire class that lived like the British royal family, but with no civil list and no public scrutiny. However, for this particular communist leader, royal style meant Liz Taylor and Richard Burton rather than the Windsors (*opposite, top*).

In the picture below, Tito is having tea in his den in his Brdo pri Kranju residence with the American film star Kirk Douglas (born Issur Danielovitch Demsky, the son of a Jewish-Russian refugee). Douglas looks ill at ease. Which publicist agreed to this interview? How did Douglas get here? There are vicious-looking flower arrangements, some dainty tea-things, an orange carpet, a rubber plant and some anonymous light-wood furniture – comfortable low chairs and a coffee table with tapered legs and an iridescent onyx top. The walls are finished with light wood strips to dado level. One thing's for sure: this is another film set.

By the 1950s, along with the New Class, Tito was living very comfortably indeed. (Tito, incidentally, was his pet name to the nation – he was born Josip Broz.) He owned public buildings and private houses. In his retreats

on Vanga – part of the Brioni Islands – and Brdo pri Kranju, this nineteenth-century (he was born in 1892) Croatian blacksmith's son and former metalworker lived in the style of an elderly German, middle class entrepreneur who has made his money in, say, cigarette-manufacturing machines and has now settled in a comfortable but socially unsmart suburb with something of 1950s America about it. Imagine that this wise old rough diamond is also in constant demand to share his wisdom in *How To* books and international conferences. So he's always out and about. In the 1960s and 1970s – the Golden Age of 'non-alignment' – Tito was forever dropping in on Nasser and Nehru, Libya and Liberia, dispensing hints and tips. He was the most travelled and entertained Eastern European leader by a mile. But as he became older and fatter and more out of touch, Yugoslavia fell further and further into debt and all those tribal hatreds came seeping back.

Everything here is in our tobacco-machinery nabob style. A first-generation completely non-Establishment décor that doesn't look back. It's all comfortable optimistic postwar Western modernity. It could be Germany in the 1960s. This is not a historic house.

Here (*opposite*) we find Tito in a corner of his kitchen, his prosperity prominently displayed in the wrought-iron grapevine wine rack with its collection of what looks like Yugoslav *blanc de blanc*. So very 1960s, so very tourist – and for display purposes only. He's brewing exotic mud-like coffee on a Baby Belling for friends, just like a real person. The background is exposed random stone reminiscent of those crazy-paving 'feature walls' in 1950s American dream homes.

Another carefully posed picture (*right*) taken in the same house shows Tito hard at 'work' in his 'workshop'. Dressed in smart overalls, he's showing us how he keeps up with his old metalworking skills (all communist hagiographies emphasize the leader's proletarian past – Tito, a man of the prosperous, aspirant people). The hobby machinery is a Myford lathe, the latest imported model from Lancashire.

All of these domestic photo-opportunities by the nation's grandad disguise the fact that this elderly man ran the toughest partisan campaign imaginable in the Second

World War and then promptly executed 30,000 people with whom he happened to disagree: pro-royalists and pro-Germans.

Here's Tito relaxing at home (*opposite*). It's beyond weird. It looks like a contemporary super-Realist photo-artist's ironic fantasy collage. The menagerie – live and stuffed – is concentrated in just a few square yards. And the maker of modern Yugoslavia, dressed in his customary bright blue suit, looks equally stuffed. (It's not such a strange idea: in his last photographs, 'Papa Doc' Duvalier, the Haitian dictator, was reputedly stuffed.)

The furniture is late nineteenth-century French-polished, gadrooned Mittel-Europa, vaguely acknowledging earlier styles. The flowers are stiff – and possibly fake – and the white china piece is practically Lladró. It's smooth, expensive, comprehensively awful and everyone knows someone who's got some – the achieved artisans' global favorite.

Beyond in the sunlit garden, through the American-style picture window, the bright-striped garden chairs show that it's the 1970s not the 1930s and that the cunning old war-hero is coasting to death (he died in 1980) and the break-up of his creation. So he is blithely sending out power, wealth and virility signals that strike a contemporary eye as completely nutty. In this picture Tito is saying he's a man of judgment. He's holding a big book too, so he's a man of taste and delicacy with not one but two flower arrangements in sight. He's also a fighter, an Alpha male, with three dead rare beasts in the corner of the room and a devoted Alsatian, the action man's dog, who must be wondering when it will be his turn to visit the taxidermist.

Tito gets about. Here (*below*) he is on the terrace of his home in Igalo – Yugoslavia's Bath. It enjoys fabulous views over the Adriatic, nestling just south of Dubrovnik in what is now Montenegro, and is just the kind of resort that made Yugoslavia such a profitable tourist destination in the 1970s and 1980s, before the troubles resurfaced. Tito is posing for a sculpture. Being constantly painted and sculpted is all part of the job for most heads of state, but especially for communist dictators – so much so that

a set of conventions evolved for these heroic heads and oil paintings. But this sculptor seems to have gone off-message. His version of Tito owes more to Tom Hanks than the Savior of the People: he has made Tito look like the Forrest Gump of dictators. For this character, 'Life is like a box of chocolates, you never know what you're gonna get.' This is consumer entertainment.

The real Tito, once again, looks more dead than alive. He's lolling back in a latter-day wing chair of the kind they sell by mail in the back of the *Sunday Telegraph* – the kind that has an extra spring-loaded piece in front to support tired legs. And indeed Tito's legs let him down in the end. In 1980, age 88, he had an operation for veins in his right foot. It went wrong and the foot had to be amputated the following week. Tito was dead a few months later, after which Yugoslavia began to fall apart.

On Tito's far side is a furled sun umbrella, but you half expect it to be his personal standard. This luxurious image gives us some idea of just how nice it must have been to be Tito in his declining years: doings things your own way, outliving your contemporaries and enjoying every modern comfort. All is well in this best of all possible worlds.

Here's the great dictator reading the newspaper on a wipe-clean surface (*opposite, top*), with a nice reproduction lacquered-brass lamp, which won't tarnish and requires no polishing. Here's a birthday lunch on the Dalmatian Coast (*opposite, bottom*). A row of pastel parasols. We could be in a 1960s movie; indeed we could be in *The Prisoner*. The highly engaged young people are Tito's Pioneers – a kind of Hitler Youth who will later be enjoined to 'keep brotherhood and unity as the pupil of our own eye'.

Tito, like all dictators, had many more abodes, including the royal palace, previously occupied by King Peter II. This palace – 'of recent construction', like the Yugoslav monarchy itself – is in an earlier style, with a variety of European origins, much of it in that rather tasteful early twentieth-century revival style (think of Sir Aston Webb's 1913 new classical facade for Buckingham Palace). Tito had the run of it and used it for major enter-tainment. He did, however, take the royal crowns off everything and replace them with symbols of the people.

Every house in Tito's collection had its uses. He was fond of dogs and hunting, so there was a house for that. And he was more than fond of women, so others served for romantic liaisons. But in our pictures, spliced together like a film – *Carry on Tito*, perhaps – we see the personal taste, the peasant-made-good taste of this apparently charming yet utterly ruthless and brutal old man.

But remember, all this Adriatic kitsch is our history too: just think Yugo-tours.

FRANCISCO FRANCO

In 1939 General Francisco Franco, victor in the bloody Spanish Civil War (1936–9), bomber of Guernica and admirer of Hitler and Mussolini, moved his headquarters to Madrid. His first instinct was to move into the Royal Palace. He was persuaded not to because it would enrage the monarchists. He went instead to El Pardo, a sixteenth-century royal hunting lodge just outside Madrid.

Hunting lodge here means 'secondary palace' rather than anything an upper-class Scot would recognize. Built in Spain's richest artistic century and constantly added to over the years, El Pardo was just the sort of place to make a profoundly conservative, middle-class Spanish dictator think he'd really arrived. It's a deeply unoriginal right-winger's idea of the *Patria*, the Spanish Fatherland.

The drawing room (*overleaf*) is a full-on red and gold affair. Paintings are used merely to decorate the panelling and there's a major painted ceiling with elaborate plaster-work (the original of the terrible ceiling features in Saddam's palaces on pages 90–4). Then there's the white and gold early nineteenth-century furniture and a spectacular carpet made for the room, plus masses of bright red damask (rather like Buckingham Palace), probably introduced by the Francos.

The dining room (*opposite*) follows the same conventions. There's a fabulous chandelier; there are pictures involving dogs and hunting (a particular passion of Franco's), gilded chairs and console tables, lamps on stands and a commissioned carpet. Living here with his cold, ambitious wife and only child, Franco must have felt he was living in a museum. Yet he stayed here for 36 years, a fascist relic in post-war Europe, until his death in 1975.

The Francos' summer house (*right*), El Pazo de Meirás, is a proper hunting lodge in the Scottish sense. The exterior looks like a castle fragment. The interior is very Spanish (*page 47, top*), yet at the same time speaks the universal language of hunting lodges: an exposed-beam ceiling, whitewashed walls and an early, over-sized

FULL NAME
Francisco Paulino Hermenegildo Teódulo Franco y Bahamonde

TITLES
'Jefe del Estado', Head of State; Generalísimo Francisco Franco

INFAMOUS MONIKERS
El Caudillo ('The Leader'); Francisco the Frog

YEARS IN POWER
1939–75

FAMILY
wife: **Carmen Polo**
daughter: **Carmen Franco Polo**

chimney piece; there are stags' heads on the walls and a giant tapestry, but no pictures. Plates are mounted on the waist-high panelling and there are simple, leather-seated old chairs. Only the carpet – a giant antique Savonnerie – looks excessively luxurious. (In Scotland it would be a threadbare, brick-red Turkey carpet.) There is also a huge marble staircase that divides at the landing level, underneath a stained-glass window – just to give visitors an impression of something churchy.

These china display shelves from El Pardo (*opposite, bottom*) with their fat gilded seventeenth-century cherubim are typical Spanish too. The plates are Kensington Church Street quality. The chairs to the side with their plain red leather seats are English 'in the Chippendale style', though they might well be 1880s Pall Mall gentlemen's club reproductions. The rug under the table looks astonishingly like a 1930s Modernist abstract.

This (*right, bottom*) is a strangely elegant bedroom in the El Pazo lodge. Plain dark walls, pleasant furniture – some of it English – the favorite of geriatric snobs the world over – a simple exposed floor with small plain rugs on it. There are also two large sleigh beds on a platform (what is it with beds on platforms?). It's all very much in keeping with what you'd expect from contemporary accounts of the Franco marriage.

It's hard to imagine the misery of staying with the Francos. The biographer Gabrielle Ashford Hodges describes Franco as 'an effeminate, inadequate individual who was determined to shroud his shortcomings behind a harsh and cold facade – an awkward skinny kid with large ears and huge mournful eyes'. General Franco was a titch – five foot three – with 'hands like a woman's and always damp with perspiration . . . the voice shrill and pitched in a high note'. He didn't have Hitler's mesmerizing ability to rant or Mussolini's easy popularity and sex appeal.

Although a Fascist dictator proper in his sympathies and alliances, Franco's instincts were always conservative, Catholic and – equivocally – royalist. He brought up King Juan Carlos as his successor. However, after Franco's death the king helped to dismantle the general's oppressive legacy as bloodlessly as possible, dragging Spain into modern Europe. He can't have enjoyed staying at El Pardo much.

JUAN PERÓN

FULL NAME
Juan Domingo Perón

TITLE
President of Argentina

YEARS IN POWER
1946–55; 1973–4

FAMILY
first wife: **Aurelia Tizón**
second wife: **María Eva Duarte**
third wife: **Isabel Martínez**

Everything's different in South America, particularly where the army's concerned. There was a time when any senior army officer knew that he might, one day, have to run the country. But he would have expected to rule as part of a junta, and only temporarily. He certainly wouldn't have expected to become dictator.

In the 1940s Juan Domingo Perón seemed to follow the pattern, going from career soldier to career politician and then on to demagogue and president of Argentina in 1946. As a military attaché in Italy before the Second World War he'd seen the Fascists at close hand. He studied the rhetoric of European totalitarianism – and adopted some of its theatricality. His presidency was orchestrated with his second wife – the glamorous Evita – and involved an alliance with the unions, set-piece speeches to huge crowds and the usual repression of liberal opposition and strong-arm tactics. Together, they were a highly successful and attractive double act.

Seen here in his bedroom (*opposite*), Perón is a tall and handsome colonel, the army's champion fencer, the lower-middle-class boy who displays the symbols of his upward mobility everywhere. He wears long boots; he clearly knows he's handsome and is radiating Hero-of-the-Regiment for all it's worth. The over-decorated room – the busy wallpaper, the flowers, the bedside table, the corner table loaded with pictures and a clock – has the feel of a dark, French provincial hotel.

In many ways, Perón resists the classic South American dictator-type. He was certainly not the conservative Catholic officer, and it is difficult to place him in conventional Right–Left terms. He instituted a program of rapid industrialization, heavy state intervention, anti-American (and anti-British) posturing and the promotion of a 'Third Position' somewhere between communism and capitalism. There was some nationalization (of the railways and public utilities) and price-setting for certain products, while political control was underwritten entirely by the military. But Perón's Argentina was hardly Castro's Cuba.

His regime was openly melodramatic and intensely personal. Wage increases and fringe benefits for industrial workers were heavily publicized. Evita set up her own 'foundations' for babies and the blind and doled out new spectacles and false teeth like some latter-day saint. In a speech from the balcony of the pink-painted presidential palace, she famously held up an arm heavy with gold bracelets and cried: 'We, the shirtless, salute you!' But people began to wonder where all the money was coming from and stories of corruption soon surfaced.

Evita had been an ambitious actress, young and pretty with high-maintenance big hair and heavy makeup. She knew all about good PR and how to pose for the camera. This whole composition (*opposite*) – the piano, the smile over the shoulder, hands resting on the keyboard – is pure Hollywood. The room is comfortably plutocratic. The grand piano circa 1910, the carefully placed photograph of Juan, the operatic flowers, the heavy-framed nineteenth-century oils and the button-backed satin-covered armchair are all from the repertoire of international early twentieth-century New Money with Old Money aspirations. Buenos Aires in the 1940s was a sophisticated 'European' city with large groups of well-off Italians and British.

Despite increasing opposition to inflation and oppression, Perón was re-elected with an even larger majority in 1951, but the following year Evita died at 33 from cervical cancer. Perón was deeply depressed and had one of the world's top embalmers preserve her body in an impressively lifelike condition while he tried to build her a monument. However, in 1955 he was deposed in a military coup. He fled to Madrid and soldiers did unspeakable things to Evita's lifelike corpse until it was secretly buried in Milan in 1957.

Madrid made sense for Perón – he had a sympathetic contemporary in Franco, another old soldier, and he and Evita had done a lot of business there just after the war. Nothing went right in Argentina for the next two decades. Successive governments seemed incapable of holding things together and 'Perónism' began to be remembered with a certain fondness. Ever since Perón had been deposed, Evita's legendary jewellery collection (*above*) had been on public display in glass cases. The soldier keeping watch looks genuinely interested.

In 1971 Argentina's military rulers dug Evita up and returned her body to Perón as a peace offering. The same year the military regime promised to restore democracy – doing themselves out of a job. Perón became president of Argentina again in the 1973 elections, but he died eight months later before he could ship Evita back to the nation. That task fell to his unpopular third wife and vice-president, the former cabaret dancer Isabel Martínez. When she was deposed in yet another military coup in 1976 Evita's well-travelled corpse went AWOL again. The family got it back six months later and had it securely buried in the family crypt – under several layers of steel.

But how did Juan and Evita get so famously rich? It emerged 50 years later that the Peróns had made hundreds of millions of dollars after the war organizing escape routes through Spain to Argentina for runaway Nazis. An estimated 15,000 Nazis sought sanctuary in Argentina – in return for a significant share of their loot. In her 1947 tour of Europe, Evita opened several bank accounts in which she stashed her Nazi gold – a detail that *Evita: The Musical* omits.

NICOLAE CEAUSESCU

FULL NAME
Nicolae Ceausescu

TITLES
First Secretary Communist Party; General Secretary Communist Party; President of the State Council; Major General President of Romania

INFAMOUS MONIKER
The Conducator

YEARS IN POWER
1965–89

FAMILY
wife: **Elena Petrescu**
son: **Nicu and Valentin (adopted)**
daughter: **Zoia**

Nicolae Ceausescu's biographer John Sweeney notes precisely when the Romanian dictator went barking mad, rather than being merely 'an unstable paranoiac'. It was during a trip he and his lovely wife Elena made to China and North Korea in 1971. Seeing the North Korean people's total dedication to their Great Leader Kim Il Sung proved an epiphany. The capital Pyongyang was, Sweeney writes, 'a city turned into a shrine, an urban monument', and Ceausescu was impressed. It put your average small 1970s Eastern European communist state in the shade. From that moment on, Ceausescu resolved to make Romania more like North Korea. He became more self-aggrandizing, even more paranoid and increasingly out of touch with the popular resentment that festered for the next 18 years.

Nothing demonstrated this better than his mad, super-sized People's Palace in Bucharest (*left, bottom*). It's gigantic – the second biggest building in the world after the Pentagon in the world's 46th largest nation by population. Clearing the site and its environs in the late 1980s meant demolishing about 7,000 buildings – including houses, schools and a hospital – to make way for a building with a staggeringly totalitarian frump of an exterior. The building program was said to have involved about 20,000 builders and 600 architects. There was a patriotic emphasis on home-sourced materials – Romanian marble and Romanian craftsmen. In fact, the People's Palace was so ambitious that it was still unfinished when Ceausescu was executed in 1989.

Ceausescu promoted himself from general secretary to Romania's first president in 1974. At his inauguration ceremony he carried a scepter – adding a touch of medieval princely style to the proceedings. He wielded it again on many public occasions. After his election as President of the Republic he tightened his control by putting trustees and family members in key party and government jobs. His wife Elena, three brothers, a son and a brother-in-law made it a real kitchen cabinet. This

development – one up from the Yugoslav writer Milovan Djilas's New Class (see Tito, page 32) – was what waggish Western wonks in the Foreign Office and the State Department called 'dynastic socialism'.

The Ceausescus – Nicolae and Elena – always looked old and crabby. Nicolae appeared deeply hangdog most of the time while his wife Elena, a true believer, looked like the Moral Guardian from Hell. There was something valetudinarian about them, an air of suppositories and liver tonics. Most of all they were neurotic about cleanliness. A doctor who tended the wounded after the devastating Romanian earthquake of 1977 described how, during a visit to a Bucharest hospital, Nicolae wouldn't shake hands with anyone or touch anything. As the presidential couple left, their chief bodyguard took out a bottle of special alcohol with which he washed their hands before wiping them with sterilized handkerchiefs.

The following year the Ceausescus enjoyed a state visit to Britain and stayed in Buckingham Palace. Britain wanted to keep the lines of communication open to any Warsaw Pact countries that defied the Soviet Union (hence all the Western support for Yugoslavia) and the Romanians, though famously repressive, had opposed the Soviet invasion of Czechoslovakia in 1968 and had even flirted with 'non-alignment'. The British government also wanted to sell the Romanians £300 million-worth of aircraft. However, during their visit the Ceausescus' paranoia was on parade. Nicolae brought a taster with him to check that the palace food was not poisoned – massively insulting to the Queen. His heavies from the Securitate, the state security force, were always on show and the alcohol handwashing routine followed any human contact, however regal. One morning at 6 a.m. Ceausescu and his entourage were seen talking in the palace gardens – he was convinced his room was bugged. The Queen didn't invite him back.

The Ceausescus' living quarters are rivetingly ugly – as taste-blind as any official building. Despite being over-scaled, they somehow look mean because they combine the worst of everything: the superannuated provincial Victorian railway-hotel look of the public rooms mixed with the old New Jersey dentist-style of the private spaces. Despite all the expensive imports, there's nothing here to

redeem the style. Everything the Ceausescus had done was the sort of stuff you'd strip out if you bought a house that belonged to a formerly successful geriatric. Their raging fear of contamination and illness is dramatized by their fascinating array of bathrooms, 'treatment rooms' and bathtubs. Clearly the Ceausescus could never get quite clean enough. What is this bath (*opposite*) with all its knobs and hoses? Were the Ceausescus early converts to colonic irrigation? Did they do it daily? The colors in this windowless Snagov Palace therapy room – the hard peacock blue of the bath, the orange of the tile edging – are early 1970s commercial bravura. They may be fashionable today as ironic color accents, but nobody *seriously* lives like that.

And what does that curious, clover-shaped stainless-steel appliance (*right, below*) from the spa room do? Does it boil people or school food? How many people at a time? What did it do for Ceausescu, a hypochondriac who nevertheless wouldn't follow his doctor's orders? He refused to take regular insulin for his diabetes or prescription drugs for his heart, which meant that, at the end, his paranoia was heightened by serious illness.

Another bathroom in Snagov (*page 54*) seems to come from the same supplier of tyrant-kitsch as Saddam Hussein's. The double washbasin is a strong lilac and the taps and all the metalwork are a bright lacquered 'gold' alloy. The bath, set in a recess, is surrounded by gold mosaic tiles. The shower-screen and stylized flowers of the wall tiles are a reminder that the vernacular Romanian style owes as much to the old Ottoman Empire as to the later imported French and German styles.

The water-feature affair with its bronze terrapin (*page 59*) is in the Ceausescus' Primaverii Palace in Bucharest. It looks even more Turkish, with its purplish mosaic and marble edge. The Frenchy gilt chair in the foreground with the overblown nineteenth-century woolwork flowers is a staple of the export furniture trade – this kind of furniture, produced in quantity for the world's New Rich for the last 150 years, is all over the Ceausescus' various villas and palaces.

There were also swimming pools everywhere. This one (*page 59*) at Primaverii manages to look institutional (square-cut, gloomy, utilitarian ceiling), Romanian folk-arty

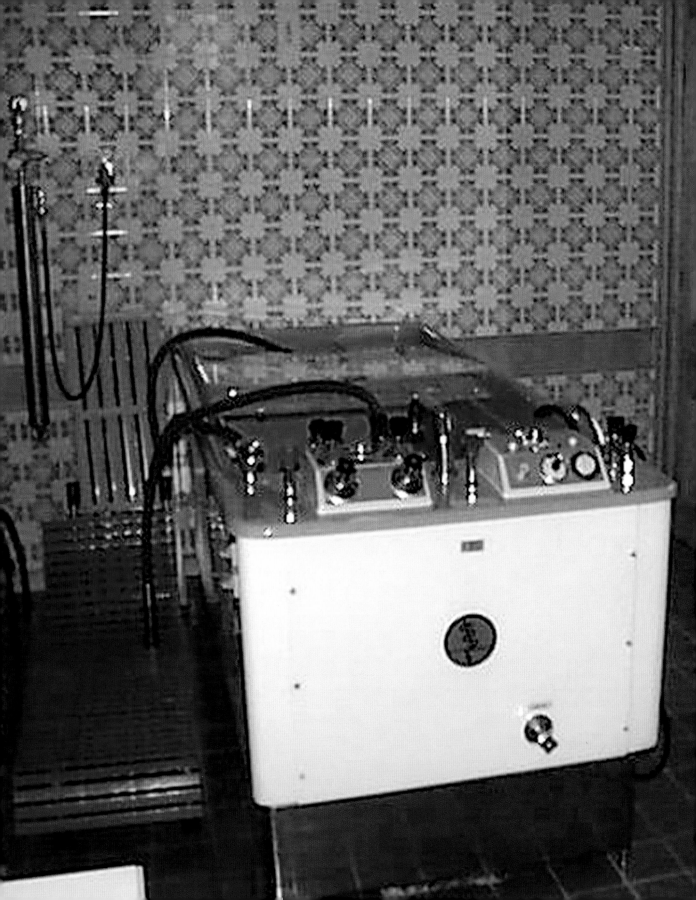

and slightly hippified at the same time. But who actually swam there? Was the pool heated? The colors are a disaster because the water looks so brackish and uninviting. There are stylized fish on the wall, rendered in deep pink (these fish probably mean something, if only someone could still read this kind of symbolism). There are birds and, no doubt in another corner of the mural, some beasts. The decorative impulse fails, however, when it comes to the chairs. It looks as if there were more spectators than swimmers here, and you can almost smell the early synthetic upholstery. The chair frames are made of square-section metal that has turned greenish from condensation. Like everything else in the Ceausescus' houses, it's a deeply oppressive space.

A third of the Primaverii Palace was given over to basement bunkers where the Ceausescus kept their flight capital: absolutely anything you might be able to turn into cash was stored here – carpets! leopard skins! (one room was piled high with them) – quite enough to cheat death forever. This head-on leopard-skin rug (*opposite*), for example – the old offensive kind – was probably a present from one of the non-aligned leaders whom Ceausescu, like Tito, often visited in his later years. But here it's just one item in the great pile of carpets and rugs – most of them the bright chemical-dyed, new-looking Persians of the 1970s and 1980s, not the soft vegetable-dyed pre-1910 kind – that were auctioned off after the Ceausescus died. Despite Nicolae and Elena's best efforts at self-preservation, these carpets and the rest of their hoard never came in very handy. No amount of pools, baths, alcohol wipes and funny hoses could save them from the firing squad on Christmas Day 1989.

Ten years later much of the contents of their homes was auctioned publicly. A chess table presented by Gary Kasparov went for $2,400, along with cars given by President Nixon (a Buick Electra), President Mitterrand and the Shah of Iran. There were rails and rails of Elena's fur coats (page 60). There were huge kitschy oil paintings exalting the couple as statesman and -woman, scientists and figures from Romanian history like Michael the Brave. Here is Elena (above the fireplace) receiving her degree, although apparently she left school at 14. Here are French gilt and ceramic clocks so gross they're practically

fairground prizes. Along with all of this there were 1,000 bottles of wine, champagne and cognac. The proceeds went to an old people's home.

Not everything was sold, however. Some of the clothes – an assortment of crocodile bags, leopard-skin purses, snakeskin shoes, minks, evening dresses and bathrobes decorated with gold thread – were given to Europe's last leper colony – in Romania. How exactly did the lepers make use of this odd bequest? And what did they do with Nicolae's 9,000 suits? Apparently he had a new suit for every day of his nearly 25 years in power. Whether out of vanity or extreme fear of contamination, that's quite something. It probably merits an entry in the *Guinness Book of World Records*. Unfortunately for the lepers, Ceausescu was only five foot two – and that's small, even in Romania.

JOSEPH-DÉSIRÉ MOBUTU

This extraordinary collection of chinoiserie (*opposite*) – the traditional pavilions, despite the new concrete walkways, benches and riverbank supports – isn't in Beijing or a theme park in Florida. This is deep in the heart of Africa, in what is now the Democratic Republic of Congo, formerly Zaire and before that the Belgian Congo. It is *The Heart of Darkness* country. From 1965 to 1997 it was the personal fiefdom of Mobutu Sese Seko, self-declared President for Life. These pavilions belong to his estate in Gbadolite, his home town some 700 miles north of the capital Kinshasa.

Somewhere on this strange campus the African equivalent of the Field of the Cloth of Gold was held. Mobutu met fellow autocrat Idi Amin to discuss yet another of Zaire's recurring crises. The two former colonial army sergeants dined together under one of these loopy pagodas. The evening was very much a media event: the tables were set with solid gold cutlery (probably from Christofle in Paris), while leopards prowled around in cages. Reporters were invited to watch the two great men eat.

Despite their elaborate frilly roofs, these far pavilions aren't entirely convincing. They look like a cross between a fanciful out-of-town office park and a resort hotel, touched up with some token ethnic styling. They were a present to Mobutu from the freedom-loving People's Republic of China, though God only knows what Mao expected in return. Apparently this estate is a perfect replica of the Forbidden City, though I'm not convinced. Like Saddam Hussein's over-energetic re-creation of Nebuchadnezzar's palace in modern materials, these buildings belong very much to their own time.

Mobutu owned eleven places in Zaire, but in the 1970s he effectively moved his world to Gbadolite. The area was linked to his tribe – always reassuring for a dictator to have family around – and it was close to Bokassa's Central African Republic, which would be handy if all else failed. He had his first palace built at the edge of the village and it reportedly cost $500 million. (This puts

FULL NAME
Mobutu Sese Seko Kuku Ngbendu Wa Za Banga

TITLE
President of the Republic of Zaire (now the Democratic Republic of Congo)

INFAMOUS MONIKER
'The All-Powerful Warrior Who, Because of His Endurance and Inflexible Will to Win, Will Go from Conquest to Conquest, Leaving Fire in His Wake'

YEARS IN POWER
1965–97

FAMILY

wife: **Bobi Ladawa**

projects like the millionaire property developer Nicholas van Hoogstraten's 'largest house in Britain' completely in the shade. Gbadolite #1 had an international airport with a runway long enough for Concorde (it landed there constantly) and extensive palace gardens modelled on Versailles. Consequently, the small village became a town with roads, banks, hotels and a power plant.

The funny little pavilion (*page 62*) looks as if it's sheathed in gold leaf – it might well be, because Mobutu could certainly have afforded it. This is actually an eccentric new airport building, oddly placed in the middle of nowhere. With a little help from international civil engineers and their new earthmovers, some red aggregate roadways and concrete curbs, the Heart of Darkness could become Stansted Airport with a twist.

In the 1980s Mobutu designed a second palace – to the south of Gbadolite. Then, in the 1990s, the Chinese government – Mobutu had kept up with Beijing ever since visiting Mao in 1970 – offered to build him a third palace in Chinese style. European visitors reported that the interiors of the Chinese pavilions were very decorative. Painted dragons, cranes and Chinese girls with pink fans covered the walls and ceilings. The rebel soldiers who liberated and looted the place in 1997 were shocked by the extravagance and one wonders why the Chinese didn't give the Zairians schools and hospitals? The Gbadolite palaces are now occupied by the army of a rebel warlord, Jean-Pierre Bemba.

Another Mobutu home, built near a lake in Goma, was modelled on a French chateau. All marble and glass. A lot of the fittings, however, turned out to be film-set trash and rather cheap. The huge chandeliers were plastic, as were the Romanesque plinths; the Ming vases weren't Ming; and the marble tables were fake. The oversized His & Hers bathrooms – one blue, one pink – were each dominated by a giant whirlpool and stacked with great foot-high bottles of scent. Five black Mercedes were lined up in the driveway.

The window view (*opposite*) gives a bit more megalomaniacal grandeur. The joinery of the woodsy window is traditional Chinese and the fountain has a touch of *The Last Emperor* about it. But beyond, through the window, it seems that some Milton Keynes District Council public

works are under way. There's also an avenue of fine motorway lighting. The terracotta lions in the fountain (*above*) look as if they could just be real, but the tiled pool around them says 'Holiday Inn procurement office'.

Mobutu's extravagance at home was matched by what he owned abroad. Despite being a very public proponent of 'Africanization', he spent a great deal of time and money in Europe and South Africa. Exactly where Mobutu's money was hidden has been the focus of constant speculation. The Mobutu portfolio apparently consisted of cash in Swiss bank accounts, shares in German and Swiss companies and a lot of property. One inventory identified nine 'palaces' in Belgium (including an office block in Brussels), two grand palaces in France, a villa and hotels in Marbella, a house in Madrid and a holiday home in the Algarve with a cellar stacked with vintage port from 1930, the year Mobutu was born. He owned other homes in Brazil, Senegal and the Ivory Coast.

In the declining years of his presidency Mobutu spent many months in his pink and white marble-colonnaded chateau in Cap Ferrat on the French Riviera. He also had a huge apartment/office in the plutocratic Avenue Foch – very convenient when shopping for luxury brands. This picture (*overleaf*) shows the International Man of Mystery in his Paris office. He's wearing his infamous outfit: an 'African' flowered tunic and the trademark leopard-skin hat – a traditional model that was run up by a little man round the corner. Mobutu's office is big on brass, a staple of dictatorly taste. The telephone stands on a brass étagère, the useful side table typical of the Mayfair short-let apartment. Mobutu's desk lamp, a heavy brass reproduction four-branch candelabra, has a shiny metallic 'gold' shade. On the desk is a green onyx penholder filled with golden pens (of which dictators are fond), a papier-mâché box and a big blotter. No clutter, and no early computer either. Behind the desk is a big, dark, French nineteenth-century oil painting and silk wallpaper in that mushroom shade found only in smart Euro-apartments then. Zaire was, of course, Francophone and the French and the Belgians (and the Americans) often gave Mobutu loans and arms.

Like Idi Amin, Mobutu started as a loyal soldier serving in the Belgian Congolese army, the *Force Publique*. He rose to the rank of sergeant major, which was as high as a black African could go. When he left the army he became a campaign journalist and, after independence was granted in 1960, he joined the new government as Secretary of State for Defense under Prime Minister Patrice Lumumba. When Lumumba was overthrown in a coup a few months later, Mobutu (now a colonel) moved in as prime minister. Mobutu was a first-generation African military coup-maker, a Cold War relic with all the classic characteristics: a life presidency, brutal enforcers, a cult of personality, a servile media and a gang of corrupt cronies.

In 1965 Lieutenant-General Joseph-Désiré Mobutu seized full power and declared himself president for five years. After 1970 he went in for a full-scale 'Africanization'. He renamed the country the Republic of Zaire in 1971 and in 1972 renamed himself Mobutu Sese Seko Kuku Ngbendu Wa Za Banga: 'The All-Powerful Warrior Who, Because of His Endurance and Inflexible Will to Win, Will Go from Conquest to Conquest, Leaving Fire in His Wake'. Everyone else was ordered to change their Christian names from the French Josephs and Patrices to something more authentically African. Place names were changed too.

The upside of this concentration of power was a temporary suppression of tribal conflicts and a temporary sense of nationalism. But Zaire's population lived in appalling poverty. The country's infrastructure – although the Belgians had a terrible record, they had built roads and power stations – was literally reclaimed by the jungle during Mobutu's stewardship of this huge, invented and constantly warring nation.

Yet Mobutu had a way with the West, from which he regularly extracted money in return for being yet another bulwark against Communism. In 1984, global economists calculated the Zairian national debt at around $4 billion. Mobutu's personal net worth was also about $4 billion. This beautiful symmetry was the measure of Mobutu's kleptocracy, which was second only, perhaps, to Ferdinand and Imelda Marcos. The African Studies Association conference claimed recently that Mobutu and his associates took for themselves up to 20 percent of the state's operating budget and more than half of the capital expenditure budget. In 1988 Mobutu said that he'd built churches, schools and hospitals with his own money. 'No,' he declared, 'I have a clear conscience. I am an honest man. I have not pocketed one dollar of the people's money.'

FERDINAND AND IMELDA MARCOS

FULL NAMES
Ferdinand Edralin Marcos
Imelda Romualdez Marcos

TITLES
President of the Philippines (Ferdinand);
Minister of Human Settlements (Imelda);
Governor of Metro Manila (Imelda)

INFAMOUS MONIKER
The Steel Butterfly (Imelda)

YEARS IN POWER
1965–86

FAMILY
son: **Ferdinand Jr.**
daughter: **Imee**

Exactly how much did the Marcoses steal? Ever since Ferdinand E. Marcos, President of the Philippines, was deposed in 1986 and dumped in Hawaii by the Americans, a small industry has developed dedicated to recovering his fortune for the Philippine government. Lawyers in America and Switzerland have tried to shake down banks in Zurich and Geneva, as well as members of the Marcos circle who held nominee accounts all over the place. There seems to be stuff everywhere: gold bars, cash and stocks, property in Manhattan, investments in Asian sweatshops. There's jewellery – mountains of it – and art.

So far investigators have only managed to claw back a measly few hundred million dollars, as well as auctioning some second-rate pictures worth about half a million dollars. Bits and bobs really.

Estimates of the value of the Marcoses' fortune vary. Some determined myth-breakers put it as low as $5 billion, meaning no more than comfortable, like the Duke of Westminster or Philip Green, the retail billionaire who employed Beyoncé to sing at his son's bar mitzvah. But the very top bid is around $100 billion, which would make the Marcoses the world's richest family. It's more than Bill Gates or Sam Walton. Back in 1986 the American congressman Steven Solarz famously said that the Marcos regime was 'not an aristocracy, not a meritocracy but a "kleptocracy"'. The U.S. House of Representatives Foreign Relations subcommittee waded through some vivid accounts of the Marcoses' spending habits: $40,000 on florist bills; a $560,000 bill for a single jewel; and a $3.3 million one-day shopping trip to America.

In the U.S. they found four commercial buildings in Manhattan as well as a wedge of prime Texas real estate, including a 7,000-acre farm and a hotel. Their possessions were huge, unfocused and vulgar; a jumbled mass of valuables hoovered up from all around the world. Even their investments seemed tacky.

The basic charge is that the Marcos regime acquired control over the most valuable parts of the Philippine economy, extracting vast sums of cash under various heads ('commissions'), then moved most of it abroad. Marcos's widow, Imelda, has a completely different version of events. She says that Marcos was already immensely rich through legitimate gold dealing before he became president in 1965. He had huge amounts of gold – 7,000 tons of it, a large part of the world's stock. So much, in fact, that he built walls out of it at home, using it as a kind of premium brick. Unfortunately he didn't tell Imelda. Always fussing over her interiors, Mrs. Marcos disliked the way the house was partitioned into tiny rooms, so she ordered some of the walls to be knocked down while her husband was away. The bricks were stacked in the garden, and an anxious Marcos wasted no time in retrieving them on his return.

This is a typical Imelda story: nutty and disarming. We know about her shoes, of course. When the incoming Aquino government audited the Marcoses' quarters in Malacanang Palace in Manila they said they'd found 4,000 pairs of shoes. Mrs. Marcos responded that this was ridiculous – she only had 1,200 or so. She's been in the news ever since, in constant press interviews and TV programs. They even say she bought George Hamilton a house. She sings popular songs, she reminisces, she defends her husband's reputation – and, for some years, his embalmed body, which she was keeping on ice, lobbying for its burial back in the Philippines. Others say it wasn't his body at all, but a fiberglass replica.

We all know what she looks like, too: tall with a lacquered black beehive and a pale, plump ageless face; bright color co-ordinated clothes in the American 1960s style; and immense shoulder pads with everything. She looks like a drag act from the *Cage aux Folles* period. She's certainly very camp. She comes across in interviews as a fabulous flake. She rattles on and on about love and beauty – she's always on about beauty – and her mission to bring love and beauty to the Filipinos and then to the world. She often draws diagrams for her interviewers: graphic representations of the Wisdom of the Universe. She sounds like a cross between Liberace and the Maharishi.

Imelda's milieu is global and epically tacky. Her co-defendant in several of the money-laundering accusations was Adrian Kashoggi, the billionaire arms dealer. She

tells the world about her conversations with Gaddafi and Saddam Hussein ('You should become a Muslim, Imelda') and her friendships with half of old Hollywood.

Becoming an international joke has proved extraordinarily beguiling, effectively deflecting any conventional analysis of the Marcoses' corrupt, brutal, often murderous and utterly indefensible regime. If the answer to the question 'What did they steal?' is 'Shoes', it all looks a bit comic and naive. In Imelda's version, Marcos was just a rich idealist on a mission.

In fact, everything suggests that Marcos started as he meant to go on, beginning with a murder charge at the age of 22, when he was accused of killing his lawyer-politician father's rivals. Marcos completed his law degree in prison (he was found guilty, but appealed and was freed in what's considered an early insider fix). From 1949 onwards, when he was elected as a parliamentary representative for his home province, he parlayed political influence for money and was a dollar multi-millionaire by the mid-1950s. He married Imelda in 1954.

President of the Philippines by 1965, he began with a typically showy program of public works, although his other key election promise – land reform – was never really tackled. By the late 1960s he was facing a very hard-Left Communist Party with a military wing and, in the south, Muslim separatists. He made the most of them. Posing as a bulwark against the communist threat was a classic tactic at the time for corrupt governments looking for American money and support. Marcos even sent Filipino troops to Vietnam. He maintained a close – and subsequently embarrassing – relationship with the United States throughout his 20-year term as president and the Marcos family spent a lot of time in America . . . shopping. The Marcoses described themselves as 'close friends' of Lyndon Johnson, Nixon and Reagan – and one of the key sources of laundered Marcos money was identified as American firms bidding for government contracts.

Marcos certainly redistributed wealth from all over the country – mainly in the direction of his family and cronies, particularly people from his home province of Iloco. He was a notorious nepotist: family members and close friends always took the most profitable jobs. At one time or another Imelda was Governor of Manila, leader of the majority party in the National Assembly and de facto Minister of Culture.

By the 1980s the economy was faltering and Marcos would disappear for weeks at a time for kidney treatment. He had his main political rival, Benigno Aquino, murdered in 1983. He became extremely unpopular at home and was regarded as a liability by America. After a snap election in 1986, Marcos lost to Aquino's widow Corazon and the Americans took him off to Hawaii. Hawaii has a large Filipino population, most of it 'Ilokanos' from his home state. They treated the Marcoses as local gods.

The Marcos style is fascinatingly garish, with some pretty odd mixtures of the best and the worst. They operated on the declared principle that their wealth and glamor were inspirational, that they taught the poor to strive for themselves, encouraged enterprise and were generally a tonic for the nation. By this standard, their limos and leisure centers, flowers and furniture, clothes and shoes all raised the national game. In the mold of the Peróns ('We, the shirtless, salute you'), they were *spending for the people.*

One story above all characterizes the Marcos style, its vanities and pretensions as well as its astonishing cruelties. In 1981 contractors involved in building Manila's new Film Center for Imelda were so pressured to speed up and cut corners to finish in time for the international opening that the building collapsed, burying workers – some said hundreds – alive in the setting concrete. Their bodies were cleared out and the story hushed up.

In 2000 Imelda was re-established in the Philippines. She had run (unsuccessfully) for Congress and two of her children were representatives in Marcos's home province, where her husband's body lay in a refrigerated vault. An interviewer from the BBC's World Service visited Imelda in her Manila apartment. Finding it hard to pitch the interview between high seriousness and gossip, he saw that her apartment 'provided an easy target for an interview that I knew would have to be carried by its irony'. He noticed that an obviously cod Michelangelo painting was flanked by a real Gauguin and Pissarro. A jug of plastic roses sat on a real French eighteenth-century commode.

Imelda's private rooms are from her residence in her hometown, Tacloban, which has been famously dubbed the Malacanang Palace of the south. It has a quality of early Hollywood kitsch. The reception room (that's *literally* what it's for) is ambitious and over-scaled, gilt chandeliered, pale blue and scarlet. There's a huge curtain-draped picture of Imelda (*page 71*) — rendered impossibly slender and European by a portrait painter a long way down the line of descent from, say, de Lazlo.

The bedroom (*pages 72, 74–5*) is equally Hollywood and totally female: the film-set fantasy of a Filipina former beauty queen born in 1929 who adored American films and their stars, a girl from a curious former colonial culture that was once Spanish, later American, and only gained independence in Imelda's lifetime. The only Catholic nation in Asia, the Philippines is a curious mixture of cultural influences. Once again, the room is over-scaled, set out for the camera, with the bed massively canopied and raised on a dais. It's all done in the favored textures and colors of new Catholic money: gold damask and deep pink satin. The bedside lamp has a curved fringed shade in a 1940s shape and is made in a paler knicker-pink silk. The bed is covered in some sort of wedding-dress fabric with the look of nylon net and a 'train' at the front. On the wall are heavy gilded moldings with a vast inset mirror — once again, the Hollywood idea of Royal Living. In the foreground are photographs of the presidential couple in mother-of-pearl frames. In another corner, by a fabric-covered table with some sort of pink floral arrangement, is a harp. I doubt Imelda could play it, but in her corny symbolic universe it probably stood for her bringing harmony to the world. There's nothing remotely comfortable or convenient in this room. How do you actually live in it?

The vast bathroom (*opposite*) must have been a long walk away. Of course, the centered bath is some sort of Jacuzzi waterjet affair, favored by the world's New Rich from Beijing to Billericay. It's got a greenish tinge and, given it's the Marcoses', I strongly suspect it's acrylic (you just have to tap them to know). The window's a Gothic pointed arch inset with what looks like nineteenth-century stained glass. The walls and ceilings certainly are panelled in shiny dark glass like an early disco (one can easily imagine Mrs. Marcos in *Regine's*). You can't see where the lighting — pinpoint clusters of bulbs — actually is. There's a nineteenth-century Frenchy mirror and a hotel-type chair covered in salmon pink. The whole thing's more of a chapel than a bathroom and it certainly wouldn't cut it in the Hamptons or anywhere where they go for the natural light and natural fabrics look. The abiding worry with this whole 'set', just like a disco, is that it won't look very good when you open the window in the morning — which is perhaps why the pretty pointed window looks as if it's fixed shut with some sort of pink light-diffusing ruffles.

And then, inevitably, there are the shoes — a central exhibit in Cory Aquino's indictment of the Marcoses, along with numerous unopened Marks & Spencer's girdles. This is just a corner of Imelda's vast shoe archive (*page 68*) — there are clearly hundreds arranged by type. We can see lots of wedges and espadrilles, with her kitten heels and strappies bringing up the rear. Did Imelda go without shoes as a child?

IDI AMIN

FULL NAME
Idi Amin Dada

TITLE
His Excellency President for Life

INFAMOUS MONIKERS
Lord of All the Beasts of the Earth and Fishes of the Sea and Conqueror of the British Empire in Africa in General and Uganda in Particular; Big Daddy; King of Scotland

YEARS IN POWER
1971–9

FAMILY
five wives recorded: **(Malyamu; Kay Adroa; Nora; Madina; Sarah)**
children: **about 30**

In 1952 Corporal Idi Amin Dada of the King's African Rifles was described by his British superiors as 'a splendid type and a good rugby player, but virtually bone from the neck up'. 'He needs,' they said, 'things explained in words of one letter.' Yet, another commander observed that Amin 'certainly isn't mad. He's very shrewd, very cunning and a born leader.' Was Idi Amin stupid or just pretending? Or did he start clever and go mad? In other words, how can we explain the extraordinary brutality of his eight years as president of Uganda? The nations that funded him regarded him as harmless, but it is rumored that he murdered his political opponents and kept their heads in the fridge so he could talk to them.

Idi Amin was a huge man. In this picture (*opposite*), he looks like an off-duty soldier. He makes the king-size bed look small. Anywhere else, that bed's pretensions would dominate. Tall, with deep-set mahogany arches and pinnacles it's an Anglican cathedral of beds. The picture above it, however, with its simpering 'modern countryside'-style, looks like a lithograph from a hotel.

Amin often said ideas came to him in dreams. For instance, the idea to get rid of the entire Ugandan Asian population came in a nocturnal vision, although it also came from long-standing animosity and thug economics – their assets could be distributed to his tribal cronies. It has been argued that Amin suffered from neurosyphilis, which advanced in later life and made him increasingly insane. He may even have died from it – though at 78, it was hardly an early death. In the meantime he fathered some 30 children. He probably lost count.

For an enormous man with an enormous family this place (*left*) doesn't look like much. It's a sort of big village house (probably ex-colonial) without any of the usual evidence of raging dictatorial megalomania.

In 1961 Amin became a commissioned officer, one of only two black Ugandans to make it during British rule. After independence he went on to become a colonel in Milton Obote's new regime. He later organized a successful coup in 1970, backed by Israel and endorsed by the British, who turned a blind eye to his brutality. Amin was now firmly installed as Uganda's ruler. The British Foreign Office considered him sufficiently anti-communist, predictable and willing for his horrendous crimes not to matter.

There was no shortage of donors and sponsors to give him this car (*right*). By the mid-1970s Amin was following a familiar route to the Middle East and receiving aid from Libya – in return for promising to Colonel Gaddafi that he would make Uganda an Islamic state. And of course there was an inevitable flirtation with the U.S.S.R. Around this time Amin also challenged Britain and the United States and broke off relations with Israel (saying later that Hitler had the right idea).

This isn't a small car – it's a big man. In the 1970s these Citroen SMs were very hot wheels indeed – the car of an International Man of Mystery. Amin is dressed like an off-duty chauffeur (and that's how the West saw him) while his wife looks like an African village girl. The car has one fascinating feature, which appears to be custom-built. The number plate is set into a housing of glass – presumably bullet-proof – that runs the width of the radiator around the triple headlights.

The carefully trimmed lawn, the well-tended hedge and backdrop of trees all conspire to make the house look like a CEO's family retreat. Behind his wife the steep traditional roof tiles over the whitewashed rendering of the house contribute to this atmosphere of moderate success. In the early 1970s Amin was regarded as a joke in Britain. He was often impersonated on TV by Primrose Hill satirical types like John Bird with his 'Ugandan discussions'. This fatally patronizing attitude meant it took years for the international community to recognize what was really happening in Uganda.

By 1972 the nationwide terror had started. Amin's record is entirely comparable with better-known mass murderers, once the generally agreed-upon toll of 400,000 killed is scaled up. His targets were ostensibly rival tribes and anyone who'd supported his predecessor Milton Obote, but they cut deep into the national structure: his own cabinet colleagues, the Chief Justice, the professional middle classes, the senior clergy – Amin killed them all.

By 1975 he was a Western pariah and Uganda's economy was collapsing. The country's most talented people had been killed or expelled and the remainder lived in terror. Uganda's budget was diverted largely to fund Amin's newly organized security forces, the sinister

killing squads that implemented martial law. Then, in 1976, there was the Entebbe hijack of an Air France passenger jet carrying 105 Israelis by pro-Palestinian terrorists. It was allowed to land at Entebbe Airport in Uganda. This was the defining moment of Amin's presidency. He cooperated with the terrorists and the spectacular Israeli commando rescue that followed left him humbled.

Impossibly, things got worse. In 1978 he attacked neighboring Tanzania, as bad a judgement call as Saddam's invasion of Kuwait. The Tanzanians counter-attacked (aided by Ugandan exiles) and drove Amin, his five wives, several mistresses and numerous children into exile in Libya. After a few months, the Libyans asked him to leave.

This (above and opposite) is Idi Amin in his final exile in Jedda, Saudi Arabia. At first sight it looks like a Peckham council flat and – to a tabloid eye – Amin's posture says 'income-support claimant'. Actually the Saudis gave him $1,400 a month, a car and chauffeur and a maid. There is shag-pile carpet, an indicator of the Western underclass since the late 1960s. Then there's the chrome-legged smoked-glass coffee table, the staple of a million transfer-income furnishing schemes.

But look more closely and remember that exile is a place where time and décor stand still. The telephone is

a push-button system that was once advanced and expensive, the tool of people who gave orders. Except that nobody takes his calls anymore. His watch with its metal bracelet is also hefty and expensive. The cut-velvet suite is horribly ugly, but equally likely to have come from Harrods or somewhere reassuringly expensive. The white Muslim robe is the modern African equivalent of a power suit and covers a lot. The stainless-steel doors look as if they might open onto a $500-a-night hotel vista. The diary in the foreground is the lightweight pocket kind, possibly the Economist's. He looks terrible, but we should remember that he meant business.

On August 16th, 2003, Idi Amin died in exile in Saudi Arabia. The following day Lord Owen (formerly David Owen, British Foreign Secretary from 1972 to 1979) told the BBC that he had suggested the Ugandan dictator should be assassinated to end the terror in his country. This idea was utterly rejected by the Labour cabinet. And yet, said Lord Owen, 'Amin's regime was the worst of all.'

JEAN-BÉDEL BOKASSA

FULL NAME
Jean-Bédel Bokassa

TITLES
**President for Life;
Emperor of the Central African Empire**

INFAMOUS MONIKERS
**Bokassa Ier; Savior of the Republic; Man of Steel;
Unparalleled Engineer; Artist and Guide of Central
Africa; Man Made to Create Nations**

YEARS IN POWER
1966–79

FAMILY
wife: **Catherine and (apparently) 17 other wives**
children: **about 62**

The one thing most people remember about Bokassa –
the late President for Life of the Central African Republic –
is his self-created emperorhood. Bokassa's role model
was Napoleon and his coronation on December 4th, 1977,
was so absurd and uncomfortable for his main paymasters
– the French political and business establishment – that it
probably hastened the day when they got rid of him.

Otherwise, Bokassa fits the African dictator profile of
the 1960s and 1970s, particularly the former *French*
colonial variety. A colonel in the French army, he seized
power after the Central African Republic was granted
independence in 1966. He then bribed and manipulated
his Western sponsors and (like Idi Amin) played them off
against oil-rich Libya and the Eastern Bloc. In addition,
there are the familiar themes of widespread internal
corruption and an absolute lack of 'governance'. But who
can forget the accusations of cannibalism? It also seems
that he fed his enemies to lions and crocodiles. And
according to Amnesty International, he beat protesting
schoolchildren to death, *himself*.

Bokassa's 1977 coronation – entirely French in style
and managed by Parisian stage designers, jewellers and
couturiers – was also French funded. The Napoleonic
theme meant eagles, laurel wreaths and the whole
Roman-world repertoire. And, of course, diamonds
everywhere – on Bokassa's imperial crown, on Empress
Catherine's crown – anywhere where they would stick.

Diamonds were a major currency for Bokassa. After
all, his country produced them and he liked to hand
them out to useful people. In a typically come-and-get-it
pose (*page 88*) he's showing off a couple of absolute
whoppers. His crucial ally and paymaster, the French
Prime Minister Valéry Giscard d'Estaing (a plutocratic
wannabe-aristocrat and big-game hunter), received
several sets of diamonds – as did his wife Anne-Aymone,
his brother Olivier and his business establishment cousins
François and Jacques. This proved very embarrassing
after Bokassa's deposition.

Bokassa's coronation was embarrassing for another reason: nobody turned up. No fellow emperors like Hirohito or the Shah of Iran, no presidents, no d'Estaing – not even Bokassa's African friends like Mobutu or Amin. There was no Pope to crown him, so he crowned himself and then crowned his empress. The ceremony took place in a basketball stadium built in the grim Eastern style – though it had been smartened up for the day by the French designer Olivier Brice, who also designed the throne (pages 86–7). Bokassa is sitting on the stomach of a gold-plated bronze eagle, 11 feet high and 14 feet wide. He's got the full works: a crown made in Paris with a blue orb and another eagle on top, an 80-carat diamond and a scepter, and he's wearing a 29-foot-long mantle of crimson velvet bordered with ermine. It's completely overdone.

The coronation cost $22 million – a quarter of his country's total budget for that year. There might have been some logic to creating a 'legitimate' rallying point for the nation and adding a bit of grandeur to a tiny country. Similarly, as Bokassa's biographer Brian Tilley has argued, there was some kind of local logic in Bokassa presenting himself as a cannibal, which implied extraordinary powers and longevity. Being a self-professed cannibal earned him real respect at home, though he denied everything after he was deposed.

Bokassa's presentational excesses and his flirtation with the Middle East meant that by the late 1970s he was more than an embarrassment to the French – he was a liability. They got rid of him in 1979. A carefully planned, French-funded coup (Operation Barracuda) reinstated Bokassa's predecessor and cousin, David Dacko. Bokassa was in Tripoli at the time, asking Colonel Gaddafi to fill up the space the French had vacated in his accounts. It was all humiliatingly quick and simple. The French took all of Bokassa's private archives – and they haven't surfaced since. Bokassa was initially refused entry to France, so he couldn't even lie low at one of his chateaux. He was packed off temporarily to Abidjan, the former capital of the Ivory Coast, until the French allowed him back in.

After that, Bokassa seemed to shrink. He was short anyway, like Napoleon, though artists always made him look tall and vigorous. In this photograph (opposite, bottom), however, his feet don't even reach the ground as he sits on an old stone bench. He is in the garden of Haudricourt Castle, one of his French houses. In 1985 Bokassa organized a tour and a press conference there to protest about his exile in France. He was, he claimed, a political prisoner.

The following year he returned to Bangui, capital of the Central African Republic, crazily expecting to be restored to the throne by immediate mass assent. Instead he was arrested and put on trial, with 14 charges ranging from murder and theft to cannibalism. His death sentence was commuted to life imprisonment, though he was released in a pardon in 1993.

The opening photograph of this section shows Bokassa at the end of his life, living in his run-down Villa Nassir, once his wife's little townhouse. He's broke, lonely, ostentatiously religious (note the crucifixes) and ill (note the bowl of pills). Two years later, he was dead.

SADDAM HUSSEIN

Iraq's a big place, but why did Saddam Hussein need quite so many palaces? What exactly was a palace for in Ba'ath Party Iraq? Was it a security measure – like all those Saddam lookalikes he used – was Saddam constantly moving from palace to palace? Were they 'consular' like, say, Holyrood, the official royal hangout in Scotland? Or were they extended family houses, like the Queen Mother's Castle of Mey?

But Saddam's home life was a world apart from that of our own dear Queen's. For a start, his palaces were mostly new-build and tended to look like hotels. As Mesopotamia, Iraq was the site of the world's first civilization, but Saddam didn't look to the ancient past for inspiration.

This Baghdad palace (*opposite*), looks like a *bad* hotel – a bad hotel in Dubai in the 1980s. What sort of architect does this stuff? Was it designed by one of those American corporate practices that do office blocks and Las Vegas fantasies and can turn their hand to anything? Or were they trusted locals who could be relied upon to do the security stuff – the deep reinforced bunkers and escape tunnels? Security was probably more important to Saddam than aesthetics. And what part did his terrible sons Uday and Qusay play in designing his palaces – or their various wives?

To get some idea of the Hussein family style, consider this. Once, when Uday killed a next-door neighbor – cutting his throat for some imagined disrespect – Saddam was furious because the murdered man had been a friend; so he got his people to set fire to his son's fleet of more than a hundred luxury cars. It's all fantastically primitive, like a gangster family bust-up in filmland New Jersey or Essex. Blood on the white carpets. It's also extremely clannish.

Iraq became a kingdom in 1921 because the British and Americans wanted a political bulwark against communism and Arab nationalism – as well as access to oil reserves, by then a massive consideration. It had never

FULL NAME
Saddam Hussein al-Majid al-Tikriti

TITLES
Chairman of the Revolutionary Command Council; Prime Minister; President of Republic of Iraq

INFAMOUS MONIKERS
Great Uncle; Lion of Babylon

YEARS IN POWER
1979–2003

FAMILY
first wife: **Sajida Talfah;** sons: **Uday and Qusay;** daughters: **Rana, Raghad, and Hala;** second wife: **Smira Shahander;** third wife: **Nidal al-Hamdani**

been a nation before and it wasn't exactly a satisfactory one afterwards.

King Faisal I was a useful ruler for the West, but the fault lines between the Kurds and the Sunni and Shiite Muslims, and between town and country, were never tackled. Faisal's grandson, Faisal II, was overthrown in 1958 and coup and counter-coup followed. The Ba'athist Party was the CIA's choice in 1964. Secular, anti-communist and apparently highly pragmatic, the new regime answered the West's needs – unlike its predecessor, which had nationalized the oil! – and Saddam became president in 1979.

Saddam eventually proved to be quite a headache for the West, which supported him with arms and intelligence for a decade and more on the basis that 'our enemy's enemy is our friend'. Saddam was a useful defense against communism, against Islamic fundamentalism (particularly the Iranians – the United States gave Saddam spy-in-the-sky satellite pictures during the Iran–Iraq war) and against oil nationalization.

Like his hero Stalin, Saddam Hussein was a rural peasant boy, the product of a paranoid village culture of violence. Tikrit was clearly more like Royston Vasey than Chipping Norton. It was family first, but the family was wildly dysfunctional. Married to his first cousin – whose brother he murdered by sabotaging his helicopter – his presidency was like putting someone with the instincts and loyalties of *The Sopranos* in the White House.

Baghdad, by contrast, had been a sophisticated city with an evolved middle class, a significant Jewish population (the Saatchi brothers' parents left in 1957) and relative prosperity, mainly because of oil. By Baghdad standards, Saddam and his people were *rough*. The three-dot village tattoo on his right hand screamed 'country boy'.

Like so many dictators, Saddam had been imprisoned, on the run and lived rough. When the British tabloids contrasted Saddam's underground hideaway where he was caught in 2003 (and more recently the U.S. prison cell where he was photographed in his underpants) with his '100 huge palaces', they were missing the point. *He's used to it*. That's why none of his hideous palaces really amounted to anything or looked as if they would last. In

the period when Saddam, with justified paranoia, moved from palace to palace – in parallel with a troupe of look-alikes in identical Mercedes – dinner was cooked and served in *all* of them nightly to distract potential assassins. They're glorified motels.

These photographs show one of Saddam's numerous Baghdad palaces. It's hideous, of course, as much new rich Arab decoration is to Western eyes. I live near the Edgware Road, London's own Gulf State, and I know this strand of taste from the furniture shops and bathroom-fittings emporiums that cater to it. Everything is gold. The metals are gold-colored laquered alloys (the patinated look just doesn't cut it here) and the ceramics are fluted and flashed with gilding. I recognize the Edgware Road look in the naff bathroom (*page 94*) with its multiple basins. Who used this room and how? Is it a kind of tribal gents? And, if not, why did they need quite so many basins in one place?

These palace are in the style of those big 1960s-in-the-1980s hotels you find everywhere in the Middle East. New Arab money has gone from marsh and desert to over-scaled development in two generations, buying a kind of taste that, ironically, is seen as very 'Low Rent' in the West. Saddam's own taste is more Riyadh than old Baghdad.

But Edgware Road style makes no concessions to contemporary fashion. It'll have every piece of new tech-nology going: air-con, plasma screens, CCTV, space-age kitchenology and every 'Boy's Toy' possible. But as for the Lord Rogers-at-home look – let alone the spare interiors of Minimalists like the British architect John Pawson – forget it. The extremes of European 'Old' and 'New' taste are completely inexplicable to this constituency.

Everything in every one of Saddam Hussein's surviving palaces is outrageously over-scaled. Every surface shines with marble so epically figured it looks fake. The style is everywhere and nowhere – somewhere between a hotel lobby with its gilding and its Louis the Something repro furniture and a more traditional Arab building. Here (*page 91*) an eagle opens its spectacular wings in multi-colored marble around the arched door. Eagles – an icon ultimately borrowed from the Romans – are a recurring theme in dictator-land. This one, despite its scale and its materials, looks crude and rather stupid. The Roman symbolism, one suspects, has come to Saddam via Walt Disney. It's startling, hideous and fascistic-looking – and it links up nicely with Saddam's amazing sci-fi fantasy paintings (*pages 95 and 96*). They're by Western artists – though no one you've ever heard of. These soft porn images are deeply sadistic and utterly absurd. In one (*page 95*) a super-snake is entwined around a sword-wielding orange-blond Venice Beach muscle-boy. The snake seems to spring from the pointed finger of a naked silicon-breasted centerfold who seems to have a white Playboy bunny engaged in cunnilingus on her. Behind her, the whole scene is presided over by a comically freakish creature from a 1950s Japanese horror film.

Were these pictures painted to order – or did Saddam somehow find them in some kind of New Jersey pervy painter's store? Either way, the profound sadism is obvious, along with some really disturbed ideas about race, sex and religion. It's the sort of stuff you can imagine in the houses of some of Jerry Springer's guests – Mr. Heavy Metal or Miss Part-time Hooker. There's an overwhelming feeling that nothing in Saddam's palaces is very clean and that none of it works properly – one imagines that the taps never work.

Like any hotel, the palace on pages 92–3 is clearly made for meetings, for deals and what the hotel trade likes to call 'functions'. All palaces perform this role at some time or another, but the old ones usually give us some sense of the family living there and their history; a strong sense that there are private quarters where a certain kind of life is led. But Saddam's palaces were unused 99 percent of the time and in this one you just expect fire doors, soulless corridors, safety notices and girls taking orders for coffee. The chairs and sofas are drawn up in a way that suggests a convention of dentists will shortly be watching a corporate video on veneers.

Despite the over-scaling and obsessive gilding, the detailing in this room is perfunctory and looks as if it's come direct from a supplier in small town America. Like hotel decoration, there's a 'feature' to distract the eye from the mostly bare walls (there are no mirrors) and the plain institutional tiles. The painted dome in the ceiling

(*pages 92–3*) – underlit with fluorescent tubes concealed behind the traditional Arabic border – is very Saddam. It harks back to Western classical archetypes, but at the same time obeys the Islamic ban on representing humans and features a gold-domed mosque. It's badly composed and badly executed. The horses look like athletic rats. The center of the marble-tiled floor below reflects the octagon above with a fierce attack of elaboration – more marble! more color! – but it still fails to give this seriously ugly room any sense of focus or personality.

Some of these photographs (*pages 92–3 and 96*) record Saddam's interiors on particular days of liberation in 2003. They show American soldiers – in U.S. mythology they're always farmboys from Iowa and black boys from the Deep South – looking utterly bemused at Saddam's houses. It isn't exactly the White House.

In this strange private 'den' (*page 96*) with exposed yellow brick walls, they've stumbled upon what look like beanbag chairs and 1970s sofas in stylized florals. It's all distinctly cheesy, but it would be utterly familiar to an American eye: it's the 1970s house of a small builder who'd made a bit of money. It can't have been what they expected.

The real show-stoppers here, once again, are the paintings. There's another of those sadistic fantasies with a kind of dragon hovering above a big-breasted blonde lap-dancer-type whose body language seems to be saying 'Take me, you big scaly brute!' The picture on the left appears to owe something to Munch's *The Scream* and even more to *The X-Files*. But who's that looking over Green Girl's right shoulder? It says 'rape' in any language. Lost in all of this is a really tiny dining table, apparently set for three, like something out of *Alice in Wonderland*.

THE SECRET REFUGE

Now this is Saddam's real home. Apparently, when he entertained visitors at one of his palaces, he only pretended to be living and sleeping there. He would actually sneak away to spend the night in a much humbler safe house. On the run after Iraq was invaded by the 'coalition of the willing', Saddam must have stayed in quite a few overground places just like this. Places that didn't attract anyone's attention. This end-of-the-line bolt-hole looks like the flat of a poor alky bachelor. There's clutter around, he's cooking for himself, and it's chaos. Everything looks makeshift – any attempt to keep up appearances has been dropped – though some essentials remain. There's a mirror so he can carry on dyeing his hair raven black – a sign of continuing presidential vigor and virility – and there's a double pack of toilet paper to the bottom left.

MANUEL NORIEGA

This is a Christmas scene (*opposite*), a Latin American festive tableau. But General Noriega's Christmas tree is as religious as a cheap window display in a second-rate department store. Who are those funny little munchkins at the base of the tree? Got up in bright 100 percent polyester-satin traditional Hispanic party dresses – the tallest one is wearing a sort of Dolly Parton wig – they make a very oddly sized family. Of course this is actually a stage-set with dolls, and given Noriega's reputation one does wonder if they're stuffed with cocaine.

Noriega, whose famously bad skin led the Panamanians to nickname him 'Cara di Piña' (Pineapple Face), was on the take from the Americans from the 1960s onwards. By the 1970s, as Commander of the Panamanian Armed Forces (which meant he got to wear a lot of gold braid), he was reportedly getting more than $100,000 a year from the CIA and the Pentagon. In 1976 George Bush, then the director of the CIA, showed him round the CIA's headquarters near Washington.

By the late 1980s, Noriega was less useful. His CIA minders had moved on and his drug connections became public knowledge in America. By 1988 he was indicted on federal drug charges and the following year the U.S. invaded Panama. Noriega finally surrendered in 1990. He was flown to the U.S. and tried on eight counts of drug trafficking, racketeering and money-laundering and given a 40-year prison sentence.

In prison, Noriega started reading the Bible. He enrolled on a 16-week Bible correspondence course, after which he asked the prison authorities' permission to be baptized. In 1992 a portable fiberglass baptistry arrived in the courtroom of the federal courthouse in Miami and was filled with water. It makes sense for the man who commissioned the tacky Christmas tableau to be a candidate for swift salvation in plastics.

FULL NAME
Manuel (Morena) Antonio Noriega

TITLES
**Lieutenant Colonel;
Chief of Military Intelligence;
Chief of Staff; General**

INFAMOUS MONIKER
Cara de Piña 'Pineapple Face'

YEARS IN POWER
1983–89

FAMILY
wife: **Felicidad Siero de Noriega**
daughters: **Lorena, Sondra, Thais**

SLOBODAN MILOSEVIC

The strong temptation with Slobodan Milosevic – one-time Yugoslav president and current Hague tribunal defendant – is to blame the wife. This colorless ex-Communist careerist and pragmatic former banker seems strangely removed from the appalling Balkan bloodbath that he orchestrated in the 1990s. He was never a charismatic demagogue for the worst of Serbian nationalism. He covered his tracks, using such a complex three-stage version of the Greater Serbian plan that killed thousands of Croats, Muslims and Albanians that it's taken the International Criminal Tribunal for the former Yugoslavia several years to pin anything on him. They've had to search hard for admissible evidence about mass graves and other gruesome details from the perpetrators themselves – the foot-soldiers – in order to establish a clear chain of command back to Milosevic. From the unofficial groups of 'militia' criminals, the concentration-camp guards, crazies and perverts (some of whom turned prosecution witnesses) to the coded instructions and the stolen money that financed their crimes, the pressure is on to prove Milosevic guilty of genocide. But Milosevic was always careful to present himself as an average apparatchik and his official house, the White House, is disarmingly boring.

His wife, Mira Markovic – with her fabled madness, her outbursts, her weird New Agery and her own blend of old hard-line Communism and Serbian nationalism – seems to have been able to change her husband's mind and strengthen his resolve with a few carefully chosen words. 'Mira has become a great leader,' Dusan Mitevic, the former head of Belgrade TV and an old crony of the Milosevices, told the BBC in 2001. 'Over the last decade his [Milosevic's] real influence has decreased and hers has increased'.

Milosevic was an apparently unremarkable small-town boy. He met Mira when he was 17 and she was 16. They went on to become a university couple in Belgrade. But both Milosevic's parents committed suicide when he was

FULL NAME
Slobodan Milosevic

TITLE
President of Serbia

INFAMOUS MONIKERS
Slobo; The Butcher of the Balkans

YEARS IN POWER
1989–2000

FAMILY
wife: **Mira Markovic**
daughter: **Marija**
son: **Marko**

a young man, and so did an uncle. This led political shrinks to read him as seriously disturbed and repressed, and the CIA to describe Mira as his surrogate mother. Nebojsa Covic, the ex-mayor of Belgrade, summed it up nicely. He said that Mira chose Milosevic, then made him president. Mira isn't just influential, says Covic: 'She's mad. It's as simple as that – and she is very powerful.' A more complex view argues that both of them are mad in mutually supportive ways – not unlike Brady and Hindley – a *folie à deux* in which two people lose touch with reality and do terrible things they'd never have done on their own. Nevertheless, their White House is a marriage of very different expectations: he wanted to look upright and statesmanlike; she just wanted to go up in the world. There are rumors that Mira designed some exotic interiors of her own – a multi-mirrored bathroom, for instance – but no incriminating photographs survive.

Then there's the White House, the former royal palace in the Belgrade suburb of Dedinje. It was built in a traditional style for the Karadjordevic family in the 1920s and 1930s. The Milosevices moved in in 1997 after he was elected president of Yugoslavia. The White House had been a busy place under Tito, but according to insiders it felt underused by the Milosevices. They made relatively little impact on it. Tito had enjoyed living it up like royalty, but he also left his stamp on the place. He changed all the royal emblems to red stars, for example.

We've seen this sort of important-looking presidential study (*page 103*) before – with Tito in it, in uniform. We're familiar with this type of heavy desk with its gadrooned edges and possibly some of this posh-trad desktop paraphernalia: the gold pen set, the silver-framed family photographs, the archaic brass blotter. The pretty nineteenth-century purply glass vase with its silver base looks elegant and the flowers are a restrained green and white. The setting is calm, spacious, unhurried – the official home of a time-server or an entrepreneurial figurehead, not the home of a pair of paranoid plotters who got neighbors to kill each other.

A billiard room (*page 107*) is something we think of as essentially Anglo-colonial, but this isn't an ordinary games room – note the orthodox-looking panel by the door (a triptych no?), the painted vaulted ceiling, and

what was once surely the altar. It's a converted Orthodox chapel. Milosevic clearly isn't too bothered by God – note the discarded cross in the corner. While some parts of the house have that unplaceable neo-neo-classical look, the original decoration here reminds us how far east we are. All of these details link to an Eastern vernacular, like the room (*above*) with a more elaborately decorated vaulting.

The wide hall (*top*) with its enfilade to the left is practically grand official Istanbul; its scalloped arches lead to more scalloped arches. The vaulting, bright decoration and central hexagonal lantern all scream not-quite-Europe, though the spindly, nineteenth-century furniture looks as if it was made somewhere a bit further West, like Vienna.

The hall (*page 109*) has more rounded arches and cool green decoration. The chairs are 1930s cut velvet and are probably royal originals, while the low table doesn't look like original anything.

In contrast, these official spaces could be in Britain – perhaps a nineteenth-century, neo-classical New Money country house. There are pale, painted walls with square-cut French panelling, symmetrically hung pictures, some nice pieces organized in received Western European taste. The chimney piece in the grand hall looks like the kind of repro-1800 fitting supplied by 'Mayfair decorators' such as White Allom in the 1920s and 1930s.

The scenic early nineteenth-century china (*page 104*) in the lit and glazed recess is nice enough, the kind of thing you'd see in secondary National Trust houses all around Britain. The chairs below are supremely English, the Hepplewhite shield-back pattern with a small English Regency-looking table between them. Good English antiques – and good English fakes – have been a default setting for international snob decorators for hundreds of years. They're more restrained, more Old Money than the ormolu and kingwood fancy French look.

The exterior is also pale and official. The style is earlier than the building itself – which was the idea. In fact, the pale stucco and portico give it the feel of a pleasant undistinguished late Regency of somewhere like the Prince of Wales's Clarence House. All is calm, all is bright.

Looking at these official rooms, you could argue that Milosevic had 'taste' – in the dull sense that they're attractively and 'correctly' decorated and furnished. They also contain some valuable pictures – the short-lived royal family bought a Rembrandt, a Poussin and some nice lesser pieces on the 1930s art market. Or you could argue that he didn't care much about his surroundings – how else could he reconcile the calm pale Western rooms with the lurid Eastern ones? Or you might feel that there's been another house altogether inside Slobodan and Mira that they'd rather nobody saw.

PORFIRIO DÍAZ
(1830–1915)

José de la Cruz Porfirio Díaz Mori was born in Oaxaca to Mexican Indian parents. He had intended to become a priest, but when the Mexican War (1846–8) began he enlisted in the army.

In the war against the French (1861–7) Díaz became something of a national hero when he led the cavalry in the Battle of Puebla in 1862. Now a senior figure in Mexico's armed forces, General Díaz became increasingly dissatisfied with the country's first president, Benito Juárez, and in 1871 led a failed attempt to overthrow the government. In 1876 he tried to oust the elected administration of President Sebastían Lerdo de Tejada, but failed and fled to the United States. He returned later that year and was finally successful in seizing power. In 1877 he was formally elected president. Díaz was a modernizing military dictator, introducing a rail network that was to span much of Mexico.

At the end of his first term, President Díaz stepped down in favor of an underling, Manuel González. But President González's administration was so corrupt and incompetent that the Mexican people welcomed back Díaz with open arms and he had no trouble being re-elected. President Díaz then set about consolidating his power by any means possible. As well as manipulating votes and assassinating political opponents, he rewrote the constitution of Mexico not once but twice to shore up his unlimited power.

In 1908, age 78 Díaz announced that Mexico was ready for democracy and free elections and he would step down. However, when Francisco I. Madero stood against Díaz, Díaz had him arrested and thrown in prison on the day of the election. It was proclaimed that Díaz had been unanimously re-elected, with Madero picking up only a few votes. This obvious electoral fraud aroused widespread anger. Madero called for a revolt against Díaz and the Mexican Revolution began. Díaz was forced from office and fled Mexico for France. He died in Paris and was buried in Montparnasse Cemetery.

VLADIMIR LENIN
(1870–1924)

Lenin was a Russian revolutionary, the leader of the Bolshevik Party and the first Premier of the Soviet Union. Born into a middle-class family, he studied to be a lawyer, but fell under the spell of Marx and Engels's *The Communist Manifesto* (1848). In 1895 he was arrested as a troublesome revolutionary and exiled to Siberia where he married Nadezhda Krupskaya in 1898. Lenin was a dynamic member of the Russian Social Democratic Workers' Party, and in *What Is to Be Done?* (1902) he outlined the party's role in bringing about revolution. This led to a split between the Bolsheviks under Lenin and the Mensheviks. In 1917 Tsar Nicholas II was forced to abdicate. Lenin then led the October Revolution, which overthrew the provisional government and established the ruling Soviet of People's Commissars under his chairmanship.

In March 1919 he founded the Third International (or Comintern) to encourage a worldwide working-class revolution. He renamed his party the Communist Party of the Soviet Union and led the Red Army to victory against the anti-Communist Whites in the Russian Civil War (1918–20). His New Economic Policy (1921) was a response to the disastrous economic effects of the war.

In May 1922 Lenin suffered a massive stroke. He died at his Big House at Gorky on January 21st, 1924. Before his death, questions had been raised about his mental stability and later there were rumors he had suffered from syphilis. Nevertheless, Lenin's legacy was guaranteed. His body was embalmed and displayed in a mausoleum in Moscow's Red Square, and Petrograd was renamed Leningrad. His model of communism – called Marxism–Leninism by Stalin – was imitated in Eastern Europe, China, South-East Asia and parts of the Caribbean and Africa. So, too, was his style of government: state monopoly, militant atheism, public terror and ideological leadership.

JOSEPH STALIN
(1879–1953)

In his Testament, Lenin called for the removal of the 'rude' Stalin. However, Stalin prevailed over Trotsky in the power struggle after Lenin's death to become General Secretary of the Soviet Communist Party. The Great Purge of the 1930s consolidated Stalin's authority. His style of dictatorship – Marxist-Leninist policies, mass repression and a 'cult of personality' – became known as Stalinism.

Born in Gori, Georgia, the son of a cobbler, 14-year-old Joseph won a scholarship to the Tiflis Theological Seminary, where he discovered Marxism. He worked with the political underground and endured numerous arrests and periods of exile. In 1912 he was elected to the Bolshevik Central Committee and soon became known by his pseudonym Stalin. After the October Revolution in 1917, he was appointed People's Commissar for Nationalities and in 1922 became General Secretary of the Communist Party, a post he manipulated to his advantage by appointing his allies to the Party.

To transform the Soviet Union into a major industrial power, Stalin implemented the Five-Year Plans and collectivization. Peasants who resisted were transported to Gulags, deported or shot. It is uncertain how many millions died under Stalin, who reputedly said: 'The death of one man is a tragedy. The death of millions is a statistic.'

After the Second World War, Stalinist governments were established in Poland, Czechoslovakia, Hungary, Romania and Bulgaria, forming the Communist Bloc. Relations between the Soviet Union and its former Western allies broke down and the Cold War (1947–91) began.

On March 1st, 1953, after an all-night dinner, Stalin collapsed, probably having suffered a stroke. Four days later he died. It has been suggested he was poisoned, but unless an autopsy is performed on his embalmed corpse, we will never know.

BENITO MUSSOLINI
(1883–1945)

Benito Mussolini was the original Fascist dictator. He was born in Predappio, Italy, the son of a blacksmith and a schoolteacher. An unruly child, he was expelled twice for attacking fellow pupils with a penknife. He was a teacher before emigrating to Switzerland in 1902 with an engraving of Karl Marx in his pocket. He returned two years later, having established a reputation as a political activist, and married Rachele Guidi, the daughter of his father's mistress. He became editor of the official Socialist paper, *Avanti!*, but was expelled for abandoning his anti-war opinions. He assumed editorship of *Il Popolo d'Italia* and, after the war, began to advocate dictatorship. An organized Fascist movement gathered around him: the Fasci di Combattimento. By late 1921 the Fascisti controlled large parts of Italy and with the country on the brink of a general strike in 1922, Mussolini declared that unless the government acted, he would. The Fascists threatened the government with their March on Rome and Mussolini was invited to form a new government. He became the youngest premier in Italy's history.

Mussolini introduced strict censorship and assumed dictatorial powers, dissolving all other political parties. His Fascist militia, or Blackshirts, terrorized the nation. Mussolini's successful war against Abyssinia (Ethiopia) in 1935–6 was opposed by the League of Nations and he allied himself with Nazi Germany, declaring war on Britain and France in 1940. As Allied troops moved up through Italy, Mussolini was turned on by the Fascist Grand Council and exiled to the mountain resort of Gran Sasso. The Nazis rescued him from jail and he briefly ran the failed Italian Socialist Republic of Salò on Lake Garda. In April 1945 Mussolini fled Salò with his mistress Clara Petacci. They were captured by Italian partisans and shot. His tomb in Predappio is now an unlikely shrine.

ADOLF HITLER
(1889–1945)

Adolf Hitler was born in Inn, Austria-Hungary, on April 20th,1889. His father – an 'irascible tyrant' according to Hitler – was a customs official. His mother was his father's niece. At 16 Hitler left school without qualifications determined to be an artist, but was rejected twice by Vienna's Academy of Arts. He eked out a living selling pictures to tourists. He enlisted when the First World War began, and Corporal Hitler was cited for bravery and twice awarded the Iron Cross. Germany's capitulation rendered Hitler hysterical and he was diagnosed as 'dangerously psychotic' by a military physician.

After the war, Hitler infiltrated the nationalist German Workers' Party as an army spy, but ended up becoming its president in 1921, renaming it the National Socialist German Workers' Party, or Nazi Party. He appealed to the nation's wounded pride and used Jews, socialists, liberals, capitalists and communists as scapegoats. In November 1923 a failed coup led to Hitler's arrest and imprisonment, where he wrote *Mein Kampf* (*My Struggle*, 1925–6). Following the Great Depression, the Nazi Party became the largest party in the German parliament and in 1933 Hitler was appointed chancellor. He quickly secured dictatorial powers as Führer, or 'national leader,' and in 1938 achieved Germany's unification with Austria – the first step in his ambition to create a Third Reich, or German empire.

Hitler instigated the Final Solution, the Nazis' genocidal assault on Jews and other minority groups, which resulted in the murder of some 11 million people. His invasion of Poland in 1939 began the Second World War, in which almost 60 million people were killed. His decision to invade the Soviet Union in 1941 and declare war on the United States guaranteed Germany's defeat. In 1945, as Soviet troops neared Berlin, Hitler – by now a trembling wreck addicted to methamphetamine (or possibly suffering from Parkinson's disease) – retreated to his underground bunker. On April 30th,1945, a day after marrying his long-term mistress, Eva Braun, he shot himself in the head.

JOSIP BROZ TITO
(1892–1980)

Tito was Yugoslavia's communist president from 1953 to 1980. He ensured that Yugoslavia, though communist, remained resolutely independent from the two superpowers during the Cold War.

Born a peasant in what is now Croatia, Tito was captured by the Russians in the First World War and became acquainted with communist ideas as a POW. He returned to Yugoslavia in 1920 and joined the Communist Party, becoming secretary general in 1937. In the Second World War he led the partisan resistance to the German occupation of Yugoslavia. By 1945 Tito's forces were victorious. The Red Army moved to central Europe, leaving Tito to shape the new Yugoslavia. Using brute force, Tito yoked together disparate Balkan territories and in 1945 he proclaimed a federal state of six republics – Bosnia-Herzegovina, Croatia, Macedonia, Montenegro, Serbia and Slovenia – modelled on the Soviet Union.

When Stalin and Tito fell out in 1948, Yugoslavia was expelled from the Communist Bloc and Tito began charting an independent course. He appeared to resolve the bitter national questions of the past (though stirrings of nationalist dissent in Croatia and Kosovo were brutally suppressed), living standards were high and his citizens were free to travel to the West, unlike their Soviet-ruled neighbors. Despite Stalin's best efforts (he even considered invasion at one point), Tito's Yugoslavia remained separate from Soviet control.

In 1953 Tito declared himself president. However, his legacy would lead to the collapse of Yugoslavia through his vicious suppression of possible successors. The Yugoslavs had a slogan: 'After Tito – Tito.' But without Tito their federation started to fall apart. Competing nationalisms began to destroy Yugoslavia, preparing the way for the Serb nationalist Slobodan Milosevic.

FRANCISCO FRANCO
(1892–1975)

Francisco Franco was born in Ferrol in northwestern Spain. His father was an officer in the navy and a drunken womanizer. His mother – to whom he was especially close – was a devout and pious upper-middle-class Catholic. Franco was unable to follow family tradition when recruitment to the navy was cut, so at 14 he joined the army. He graduated from the Toledo Infantry Academy in 1910 and was sent to fight in Morocco, which offered the chance of active service and therefore promotion. His strength as a disciplinarian and his commitment to his troops were noted and Franco began to rise through the military ranks, becoming the youngest major in the Spanish army and, by 1926, the youngest general in Spain.

When the Spanish monarchy fell in 1931, Franco kept his distance from the new Republic. However, his successful campaign to crush a miners' rebellion in Asturias (in which he employed the brutal tactics he had learned in Morocco) led to him being given the top job in the army: Chief of the General Staff. Nevertheless, he remained aloof from any plots to overthrow the Republic until a failed coup attempt degenerated into the Spanish Civil War.

In 1936 Franco became Generalissímo of the Nationalist Army and was later elected Head of State. The war ended in 1939 after the conquest of Madrid and Franco continued to rule Spain until his death in 1975. His brutality during the civil war is legendary. Tens of thousands of Republicans and their sympathizers were slaughtered in the name of Nationalism. The civil war had economically crippled Spain, but it was to be further isolated by the international community because of Franco's conduct.

In 1947 he proclaimed Spain a monarchy; in 1969 he named his successor, Prince Juan Carlos de Borbón. Franco ruled with an iron fist until he eventually mellowed. In the 1960s and 1970s Spain made economic progress. Franco died in 1975.

JUAN PERÓN
(1895–1974)

Juan Domingo Perón attended military school at the age of 16 and worked his way up through the ranks. In 1929 he married Aurelia Tizón (who died from cancer in 1942). Perón gained first-hand experience of Fascism in Italy, where he served as a military observer in the late 1930s.

In 1943 Colonel Perón was involved in a military coup against the civilian government of Ramón Castillo. Perón became Under-Secretary for War and finally Vice President and Secretary for War in 1944. He worked hard to gain popular support through his advocacy of the *descamisados* ('shirtless ones') – Argentina's underprivileged.

In 1945 Perón married Eva Duarte, an actress known by the affectionate diminutive Evita. In October 1945 Colonel Perón was arrested and forced to resign by opponents in the armed forces. Mass demonstrations organized by Argentina's trade unions and the charismatic Evita forced his release.

Popular support gained him the presidency with 56 percent of the vote in the 1946 elections and he ruled for nine years. (Evita died from cancer in 1952.) Economic problems, high levels of corruption and conflict with the Roman Catholic Church eventually contributed to Perón's overthrow in 1955. He lived in exile in Madrid, where he married the nightclub singer Isabel Martínez.

Argentina went through frequent changes of government, until in 1973 Perón became president again, with Isabel as vice president. However, his rapturous welcome was short-lived when it became clear he had changed allegiance from the Left to the Right. Upon his death in 1974, his deeply unpopular wife succeeded him. Isabel was overthrown in 1976 and replaced with a military junta. Evita and Juan Perón are probably most famous for the way their bodies were treated after death. Evita's embalmed body was buried in Italy, then Spain and then returned to Argentina. Juan's corpse was profaned in 1987 when his hands were stolen. Nobody knows who did it – or why.

NICOLAE CEAUSESCU
(1918–1989)

Nicolae Ceausescu was Romania's Communist Party leader from 1965 until he was overthrown and killed in a revolution in December 1989. He married Elena Petrescu in 1946. In 1974 he added 'General President of Romania' to his titles.

Ceausescu's relationship with the Soviet Union was complex. He ended Romania's participation in the Warsaw Pact and refused to take part in the 1968 invasion of Czechoslovakia. Romania was also one of the first countries of the Eastern Bloc to have official relations with the European Community and one of only two communist-ruled countries to take part in the 1984 Summer Olympics. On the domestic front, however, Ceausescu followed a Stalinist path. He maintained firm control over the media and tolerated no internal opposition and his secret police (Securitate) ensured that freedom of speech was ruthlessly monitored.

Ceausescu borrowed heavily from the West to finance his economic development programs. Between 1980 and 1989 he brought Romania's economy to a standstill in an attempt to eradicate the country's foreign debts. He ordered the export of much of Romania's industrial and agricultural production. The resulting domestic shortages led to rationing and gas and electricity blackouts.

Throughout 1989 Ceausescu became increasingly isolated. When he gave orders for the military, police and Securitate to open fire on anti-government demonstrators in Timisoara on December 17th,1989, it led to even more violent demonstrations in Bucharest. On December 25th, Nicolae and Elena Ceausescu were tried on charges from illegal gaining of wealth to genocide. On the same day as they were convicted, they were executed by a firing squad. One of the nervous guards accidentally shot Ceausescu in the foot before finishing him off.

JOSEPH-DÉSIRÉ MOBUTU
(1930–1997)

Joseph-Désiré Mobutu was born in Lisala, the Belgian Congo. He joined the Force Publique – the Belgian Protestant Congolese Army – in 1949 and was promoted to sergeant major. In 1958 he joined the nationalist Mouvement National Congolais and, after the granting of Congolese independence in June 1960, joined the new government as Secretary of State for Defense. When Prime Minister Patrice Lumumba and President Joseph Kasavubu began to struggle for overall power, a coup d'état overthrew Lumumba. Colonel Mobutu, a key figure in the coup, was rewarded with rapid promotion. In 1965 he seized power from President Kasavubu. He was elected president in 1970 and renamed the country the Republic of Zaire in 1971. The following year he renamed himself Mobutu Sese Seko Kuku Ngbendu Wa Za Banga (The All-Powerful Warrior Who, Because of His Endurance and Inflexible Will to Win, Will Go from Conquest to Conquest, Leaving Fire in His Wake).

Fiercely anti-European and determined to promote African independence, Mobutu nationalized all foreign-owned firms. This forced European investors out of the country, sending Zaire into an economic slump while he amassed a personal wealth of grotesque proportions. In 1984 he was estimated to be worth $4 billion – equivalent to the national debt at the time. He owned palaces in Zaire, Morocco, South Africa, France, Belgium and Switzerland.

Mobutu openly supported the Rwandan Hutu extremists responsible for the Rwandan genocide in 1994 and, in 1996, he ordered all Tutsis to leave Zaire on penalty of death. The Tutsis erupted in rebellion. With the support of President Kagame of Rwanda and Zaïrean opponents of Mobutu they launched an offensive to overthrow him. On May 16th,1997, they captured Kinshasa, and Zaire was renamed the Democratic Republic of Congo. Mobutu went into temporary exile in Togo and Morocco, and Laurent-Désiré Kabila became the new president. Mobutu died from prostate cancer in Rabat, Morocco, that same year.

FERDINAND MARCOS
(1917–1989)
IMELDA MARCOS
(1929–)

Ferdinand Marcos was the son of a lawyer-turned-politician. He was a brilliant law student at university, where he also proved himself as an exceptional marksman. In 1937 he was accused of assassinating one of his father's political rivals, but he defended himself in court and was acquitted.

This young lawyer became an aide to Manuel Roxas, the country's first president after independence, then senate president (1962–5). Meanwhile, Imelda spent her youth competing as a beauty queen and was voted Miss Manila in 1950. It was as Miss Manila that she caught the eye of Ferdinand Marcos. They married in 1954 after a famously whirlwind (11-day) romance. Imelda helped her husband in his 1965 presidential campaign. She became his closest advisor and he appointed her Minister of Human Settlements and Governor of Metro Manila.

After a promising first term, things turned sour. Ferdinand warned of an imminent communist takeover and declared martial law. He commandeered businesses, property and finances and handed them over to his friends, while ruthlessly crushing all political opposition. However, it was the couple's insatiable desire for wealth and possessions that established their reputation as kleptocrats. Approximately $684 million mysteriously disappeared from the Filipino treasury during Ferdinand's presidency.

In 1983 Benigno Aquino, leader of the opposition, was assassinated. Support gathered around Aquino's widow, Corazon, and both she and Ferdinand declared themselves the winners of a snap election in 1986. Corazon Aquino became president and the Marcoses were driven into exile in Hawaii. After Ferdinand's death in 1989, Imelda returned to the Philippines and stood for presidential election in 1992. She was defeated, but won a seat in the Philippine House of Representatives in 1995. In 2001 she was arrested on charges of corruption and extortion. Ferdinand Marcos's body was embalmed (see above).

IDI AMIN
(1928–2003)

Idi Amin was light heavyweight boxing champion of Uganda from 1951 to 1960 and a skilled careerist. He was not formally educated but rose quickly through the military ranks, joining the King's African Rifles in 1943. He served in Kenya during the Mau Mau Uprising (1952–6) and was one of the few black Africans to be made an officer before Ugandan independence. By 1968 he was Major General and Commander of the Army and Airforce.

Amin helped his close ally President Milton Obote gain power, but Obote grew suspicious of Amin's influence and had him placed under house arrest in 1970. However, in 1971 – while Obote was abroad – Amin led a military coup, aided by Britain and Israel, and seized power.

Amin was a despotic ruler renowned for his violent mood swings. Soon after coming to power he established 'killer squads' to track down and murder Obote's supporters, as well as the Ugandan intelligentsia, whom he mistrusted. Despite Uganda's relatively small Muslim population Amin declared Uganda a Muslim state. Switching allegiance from the Israelis to the Palestinians, Amin assisted the Palestinian hijackers of a French Airbus in 1976, further alienating him from his former allies. Uganda's air force was badly crippled when its fighter jets were destroyed during Israel's rescue operation.

Amin's actions at home were equally divisive and destructive. In 1972 he gave Uganda's 70,000 Asian-born citizens with British passports 90 days to leave the country. Also, his persecution of particular tribes – most notably the Acholi and Lango – provoked his downfall. In October 1978 Amin ordered the invasion of Tanzania, but the Tanzanians began a counter-attack, aided by Ugandan exiles. Amin fled the capital, Kampala, in April 1979. He found asylum in Saudi Arabia, where he lived until his death in August 2003.

During Amin's reign it is estimated that he killed 400,000 people.

JEAN-BÉDEL BOKASSA
(1921–1996)

Jean-Bédel Bokassa was born in Bobangi, Moyen-Congo, in the Central African Republic, then called French Equatorial Africa. He enlisted in the French army and earned a Légion d'Honneur and Croix de Guerre in the Second World War. In 1964 Captain Bokassa joined the army of the Central African Republic, becoming a colonel and then chief of staff of the armed forces.

Bokassa led a successful coup d'état in 1966, deposing the autocratic President David Dacko. He became President of the Republic and then restyled himself President for Life. In 1976 Bokassa declared the republic a monarchy and renamed it the Central African Empire. He converted back to Catholicism (after a brief stint as a Muslim) and crowned himself Emperor Bokassa I. His ostentatious coronation (modelled on Napoleon's) in 1977 took place in the Palais des Sports Jean-Bédel Bokassa on Bokassa Avenue, next to the Jean-Bédel Bokassa University. It was a misguided attempt to bring myth, tradition and legitimacy to his fragile regime and reputedly cost a third of the nation's $70 million annual budget. Meanwhile, the country slid further into dictatorship. Bokassa imprisoned, tortured and murdered his opponents.

In May 1979 Amnesty International published details of a massacre of about 100 children who refused to wear government-regulation uniforms. Bokassa was involved and it was even claimed he ate some of the bodies. A bloodless coup in September, while Bokassa was abroad, reinstated President Dacko. In 1986 Bokassa returned from exile. He was arrested for treason, murder, cannibalism and embezzlement and sentenced to death, but in 1988 this was commuted to life imprisonment. In 1993 President André Kolingba declared a general amnesty for all prisoners and Bokassa was released. He died of a heart attack in 1996.

SADDAM HUSSEIN
(1937–)

Saddam Hussein was President of Iraq from 1979 to 2003, when he was overthrown by a U.S.-led invasion. He joined the revolutionary Ba'ath Party in 1957. The following year a military coup led by General Abdul Karim Qassim overthrew King Faisal II of Iraq. The Ba'athists opposed this new government and, in 1959, Saddam was involved in an attempt to assassinate Prime Minister Qassim. He fled to Syria, then Egypt, and was sentenced to death in absentia. The Ba'athists came to power in a military coup in 1963 but were swiftly overthrown, which led to Saddam's imprisonment in 1964. He escaped in 1967 and became one of the leading members of the Ba'ath Party. In 1968 a second coup brought the Ba'athists back to power. Saddam became Vice Chairman of the Iraqi Revolutionary Council and Vice President of Iraq. When an ailing President Ahmad Hasan al-Bakr resigned in 1979, Saddam took over.

Saddam Hussein crushed all opposition, employing a vicious secret police network to silence dissenters. His suppression of Shiite and Kurd uprisings caused thousands to flee Iraq and even more to disappear entirely. Saddam also asserted absolute control culturally, forcing artists, musicians and architects (as well as journalists and broadcasters) to promote his iconic status.

The invasion of Iran's oil fields in 1980 led to the Iran–Iraq War (1980–88), and invading Kuwait in 1990 led to the first Persian Gulf War in 1991. The second Persian Gulf War culminated in his overthrow when Baghdad fell to U.S. forces on April 9th, 2003. Saddam fled and his sons and political heirs, Uday and Qusay, were killed by U.S. forces in July. On December 13th, 2003, U.S. troops found Saddam hiding in an underground 'spider hole' at a farmhouse in ad-Dawr near his hometown of Tikrit. He currently awaits trial for alleged war crimes, crimes against humanity and genocide.

MANUEL NORIEGA
(1938–)

Panamanian general and de facto military leader of Panama from 1983 to 1989, Noriega was raised by a relative he referred to as Mama Luisa. He had been abandoned by his parents before he was five. He grew up in Terraplén, a poor district of Panama City. On graduation from high school he noted in his yearbook that his ambition was to be 'President of the Republic'.

Noriega won a scholarship to study engineering at the Military School of Chorrillos in Lima, Peru, and returned in the early 1960s to join Panama's National Guard where he met Captain Omar Torrijos. It has been alleged that Noriega was part of the military coup that removed Panama's President Arnulfo Arias from power in 1968. His involvement probably led to the rape case he was about to stand trial for being dropped. Torrijos promoted Noriega to lieutenant colonel and appointed him chief of military intelligence. When Torrijos conveniently died in a plane crash in 1981, Noriega became chief of staff, then promoted himself to general and seized power. He is said to have been in the pay of the CIA from the late 1950s onwards, but his support of U.S. governments – the Nixon presidency in particular – was marred by persistent rumors of involvement in drug trafficking.

General Noriega was the most feared man in Panama, famous for his brutal repression of any opposition. His punishments ranged from baking prisoners naked in the midday sun until their skin bubbled to forcing soldiers to eat their own testicles and, most notoriously, to the beheading of Hugo Spadafora, Noriega's most vociferous opponent. Spadafora's head was found in a U.S. mail bag and his body discovered with 'Domestic: U.S. Mail' written on it. This, combined with Noriega's links to drugs and money laundering forced the United States to do something. When a 1989 coup failed to unseat him, the Americans invaded. Noriega surrendered on January 3rd, 1990. He was tried in the United States in 1992 and convicted of money laundering, drug trafficking – cocaine in particular – and racketeering. He is eligible for parole in 2006.

SLOBODAN MILOSEVIC
(1941–)

Slobodan Milosevic was born in Pozarevac in Serbia in 1941. His deeply religious father left his communist mother when Milosevic was four. He joined the Communist Party when he was 18. By the time he was 33, both his parents had committed suicide.

When Tito died the Communist federation of Yugoslavia began to collapse; Milosevic took full advantage of its decline. He worked the party system until he became President of the Belgrade City Committee of the League of Communists. He was promoted to Head of the Serbian Communist Party in 1986. His mentor and godfather Ivan Stambolic became President of Serbia in September 1987, but in December Milosevic forced him to resign.

Once Milosevic became president (in 1989) he set about securing the former states that had made up Yugoslavia, either by co-opting their local parliaments or through military action: the Croatian War (1991), the Bosnian War (1992–5) and the Kosovo War (1998–9). In his attempts to annex Bosnia, Croatia and Kosovo and expel their Muslim populations, Milosevic oversaw the introduction of prisoner-of-war camps in Omarska, Keraterm and Trnopolje. He also ordered the destruction of Vukovar, where more than 200 Croats were massacred in 1991. In Srebrenica in 1995, more than 8,000 Muslim men and boys were killed. That same year Milosevic signed the Dayton Peace Accord, which brought an end to the war in Bosnia. He was briefly regarded by the West as a Balkan peacemaker.

In 1999, NATO began aerial attacks against the Serbs. In 2000 Milosevic called elections, but then refused to recognize the victory of the opposition leader Vojislav Kostunica. Protesters took to the streets, storming parliament and the state TV station and setting them on fire. In 2001 Milosevic was arrested on charges of abuse of power and corruption. He is currently standing trial at the International Criminal Tribunal for the Former Yugoslavia at the Hague.

PICTURE CAPTIONS AND CREDITS

Frontispiece p.ii Statue of Stalin after it was sold to a Czech-American. The proceeds went to a local hospital © Chris Niedenthal//Time Life Pictures/Getty Images **p.vi** Portrait of Hitler hanging in Eva Braun's room © Heinrich Hoffman/ Bayerische StaatsBibliotek

DÍAZ
pp. 2–3 Porfirio Díaz's room aboard his private train, 1898 © Bettmann/Corbis

LENIN
p. 5 The dining room in Vladimir Lenin's flat in the Kremlin © Vladimir Musaelyan/ITAR-TASS (1980)

p. 6 Lenin's bedroom in the Kremlin © Alexey Stizhin/ITAR-TASS (1960)

p. 7 The living room in Lenin's flat in the Kremlin © ITAR-TASS

p. 8 Lenin's room in the Big House at Gorky © Vasily Egorov/ITAR-TASS (1966)

STALIN
p. 10 The house where Joseph Stalin was born in Gori, Georgia, before it was covered by a large marble portico in 1936 © Corbis

p. 11 Exterior of Stalin's dacha at Kholodnaya Rechka, near Gagra © ITAR-TASS

p. 13 (top) Exterior of Stalin's dacha at Zelyenaya Roshcha, which is now a hotel. Rooms cost several hundred U.S. dollars a night © Vladimir Gurin/ITAR-TASS (1996)

p. 13 (bottom) Stalin reclines on a daybed © David King collection

p. 14 (top) A desk set presented to Stalin by the Chinese communist leader Mao Tse Tung © Gumar/ITAR-TASS (1996)

p. 14 (bottom) Negotiating hall in Stalin's bunker in Kuybyshev, Samara © Nicolay Nikitin/Photo ITAR-TASS

MUSSOLINI
p. 16 Benito Mussolini, photographed at his desk in his headquarters in Rome in February 1931 © Corbis

pp. 18–19 (and p. 17 detail) Mussolini's office © Armando Bruni/Alinari (1920–40)

pp. 20–21 The cradle of Romano Mussolini, Mussolini's youngest son © Armando Bruni/Alinari (1927)

HITLER
All the images are of Adolf Hitler's alpine retreat, The Berghof, in the hamlet of Obersalzburg, 2 km from Berchtesgaden.

p. 23 Hitler's study on the first floor © Heinrich Hoffman/Bayerische StaatsBibliothek

p. 24 (top) The drawing room © Heinrich Hoffman/Bayerische StaatsBibliothek

p. 24 (bottom) A globe and a Gobelin tapestry from the Great Room © Heinrich Hoffman/Bayerische StaatsBibliothek

pp. 26–7 Porcelain figures in the drawing room © Heinrich Hoffman/Bayerische StaatsBibliothek

p. 29 (top) The living room prior to extensive refurbishment in 1935 © Heinrich Hoffman/Bayerische StaatsBibliothek

p. 29 (bottom) The parlor with basket chair © Heinrich Hoffman/Bayerische StaatsBibliothek

p. 30 Vaulted hallway © Heinrich Hoffman/Bayerische StaatsBibliothek

p. 31 Bunker emergency exit © Heinrich Hoffman/Bayerische StaatsBibliothek

TITO
pp. 33–4 Josip Broz Tito at home in his official residence in Belgrade © Bettmann/Corbis

p. 35 (top) Tito greets films stars Elizabeth Taylor and Richard Burton in one of his summer residences © Keystone/Hulton Archive/Getty Images

p. 35 (bottom) Tito having tea, chatting to Kirk Douglas in Brdo pri Kranju*

p. 36 Tito making coffee for friends*

p. 37 Tito working with a router in his workshop on Vanga*

p. 38 Tito enjoying reading*

p. 39 Tito posing for a statue at his home in Igalo*

p. 41 (top) Tito reading a newspaper*

p. 41 (bottom) Tito celebrating his birthday with Pioneers*

* Images are from www.titoville.com

FRANCO
p. 42 One of the three square towers of El Pazo de Meirás, Fransisco Franco's summer residence © EFE

p. 43 The private dining room of El Pardo, the royal palace, which contains important works of art such as the tapestries, Gaspar Becerra frescoes, and an extensive collection of neoclassical furniture © EFE/aa

pp. 44–5 El Pardo's council room and Franco's office, with Bayeux frescoes and a collection of tapestries from the Royal Tapestry Factory © EFE

p. 46 (top) The hall and staircase, El Pazo de Meirás © Miguel Cortes/EFE

p. 46 (bottom) The main bedroom, El Pazo de Meirás © Miguel Cortes/EFE

p. 47 (top) The dining room, El Pazo de Meirás © Miguel Cortes/EFE

p. 47 (bottom) Plates in the dining room at El Pardo, from www.generalisimofranco.com

PERÓN
p. 48 Juan Perón as a young man © Bettmann/Corbis

p. 50 Buenos Aires: the trinkets include a diamond necklace said to be valued at $428,000 and another diamond necklace worth $214,000 © Bettmann/Corbis

p. 51 Eva Perón playing the piano in her home © Bettmann/Corbis

CEAUSESCU
p. 52 Nicolae Ceausescu and his wife, Elena, eating a lavish dinner (undated photograph from their family album) © Corbis Sygma

p. 53 (top) Ceausescu cuts a large barbecued pig (undated photograph from the family album) © Corbis Sygma

p. 53 (bottom) House of the People, Bucharest, Romania © Michel Euler/Associated Press

p. 54 The lilac bathroom, Snagov Palace*

p. 55 The gold bathroom, Primaverii Palace*

p. 56 (top), p. 57 The therapy room, Snagov Palace*

p. 56 (bottom) Spa room, Snagov Palace*

p. 58 Carpets, Primaverii Palace*

p. 59 (top) Swimming pool, Primaverii Palace*

p. 59 (bottom) Terrapin pool, Primaverii Palace*

p. 60 Fur coats and clocks from the week-long auction of the Ceausescus' personal belongings © Radu Sigheti/Reuters/Corbis

p. 61 (top and bottom) Buyers and organizers look at some of the 650 objects formerly belonging to the Ceausescus © Radu Sigheti/Reuters/Corbis

* Images are from Ceausescu's Fortune website, www.apps.ines.ro

MOBUTU

p. 62 The airport building of Joseph-Désiré Mobutu's palace at Gbadolite, Congo © Roland Coutas/Corbis Sygma

p. 63 Mobutu's palace at Gbadolite, Congo © Roberto Antonetti/Corbis Sygma

p. 64 Mobutu's palace at Gbadolite, Congo © Roberto Antonetti/Corbis Sygma

p. 65 (top) Mobutu's palace at Gbadolite, Congo © Roberto Antonetti/Corbis Sygma

p. 67 Mobutu makes a phone call in his Avenue Foch office in Paris © Patrick Robert/Sygma/Corbis

MARCOS

p. 68 Some of the 2,500 shoes of Imelda Marcos, filed on racks in the presidential palace © Reuters/Corbis

p. 71 A mural of Imelda Marcos rising from the sea adorns the main hall of the Santo Niño shrine. When Imelda built the mansion in 1981 in her hometown of Tacloban, it was dubbed by many as the Malacanang presidential palace of the south © Romeo Gacad/AFP/Getty Images

p. 72 Imelda Marcos's bedroom © Romeo Gacad/AFP/Getty Images

pp. 74–5 Imelda Marcos's bedroom © Romeo Gacad/AFP/Getty Images

p. 76 Imelda Marcos's bathroom, with Jacuzzi © Romeo Gacad/AFP/Getty Images

AMIN

p. 78 Idi Amin sitting on his bed © Camerapix

p. 79 Exterior of Amin's house in Uganda © Camerapix

pp. 80–81 Amin standing next to his Citroen SM © Camerapix

pp. 82–3 Amin on the phone in exile in Jeddah © Camerapix

BOKASSA

p. 84 Former dictator Jean-Bédel Bokassa at home in Bangui © Riccardo Orizio/Corbis Sygma

pp. 86–7 Bokassa after crowning himself Emperor in 1977 © Pierre Guillard/AFP/Getty Images

p. 88 (top) Bokassa holds up a large jewel © Richard Melloul/Corbis/Sygma

p. 88 (bottom) Bokassa outside his residence at Haudricourt Castle where he organized a tour and press conference to protest against his conditions of exile in France © Jacques Pavlovsky/Sygma/Corbis

HUSSEIN

p. 91 A marble falcon in one of Saddam Hussein's Baghdad palaces © Jassim Mohammed/Associated Press

pp. 92–3 U.S. soldiers mill around inside the ballroom of one of Hussein's former palaces © Brennan Linsley/Associated Press

p. 94 The gold-finish fittings of a bathroom in the seized presidential palace of Basra © Simon Walker/Reuters

p. 95 A fantasy painting hangs on the wall in one of Hussein's safe houses © John Moore/Associated Press

p. 96 (top) A U.S. army captain and his men enter one of Hussein's safe houses in Baghdad © John Moore/Associated Press

p. 96 (bottom) A fantasy painting found in one of Hussein's safe houses © John Moore/Associated Press

p. 99 The makeshift kitchen in the hut where Hussein lived before he was captured in Ad Dawr, near his hometown of Tikrit © Mauricio Lima/AFP/Getty Images

NORIEGA

pp. 100–101 A U.S. soldier contemplates a Christmas tree in the former home of Manuel Noriega © Bill Gentile/Corbis

MILOSEVIC

All Slobodan Milosevic images are of The White House in Belgrade © Dragan Kujundzic. No further details were available.

BRIEF LIVES

Díaz Portrait photograph © Hulton Archive/Getty Images

Lenin A Second World War Russian propaganda poster from 1944. The text reads: 'Under the Flag of Lenin, for our Motherland, to Victory!' © Laski Diffusion/Getty Images

Stalin See frontispiece credit

Mussolini The Italian dictator sitting at his desk, stroking his cat © Time Life Pictures/Getty Images

Hitler Portrait of Hitler hanging in Eva Braun's room © Heinrich Hoffman/Bayerische StaatsBibliothek

Tito Contemporary postage stamp

Franco Contemporary postage stamp

Perón Time cover, 1951 © Time Life Pictures/Getty Images

Ceausescu The Romanian dictator poses casually beside blooming geraniums on the porch of his villa near Bucharest, August 1989 © Peter Turnley/Corbis

Mobutu The president makes a phone call in his Avenue Foch office in Paris © Patrick Robert/Sygma/Corbis

Marcos The embalmed body of Ferdinand Marcos is seen through a sealed glass coffin in a dimly-lit mausoleum in his northern Philippine hometown of Batac, September 1993 © Romeo Gacad/AFP/Getty Images

Amin Photograph of Idi Amin © Getty Images

Bokassa The coronation of Emperor Bokassa I, 1977 © Corbis/Sygma

Hussein Iraqi banknote

Noriega General Manuel Noriega under the influence of cocaine at a social gathering © Greg Smith/Corbis

Milosevic Shreds of a Slobodan Milosevic campaign poster © Eric Cabanis/AFP/Getty Images